CRAIG & FRED

CRAIG
& FRED

A MARINE, A STRAY DOG,
AND HOW THEY
RESCUED EACH OTHER

CRAIG GROSSI

wm

WILLIAM MORROW
An Imprint of HarperCollins*Publishers*

HarperCollins books may be purchased for educational, business, or sales promotional use. For information, please email the Special Markets Department at SPsales@harpercollins.com.

A hardcover edition of this book was published in 2017 by William Morrow, an imprint of HarperCollins Publishers.

FIRST WILLIAM MORROW PAPERBACK EDITION PUBLISHED 2018.

Designed by Bonni Leon-Berman

Library of Congress Cataloging-in-Publication Data has been applied for.

ISBN 978-0-06-269339-6

18 19 20 21 22   LSC   10 9 8 7 6 5 4 3

For a brief time in my life I walked among giants.

This book is dedicated to those I walked alongside—

to those who made it back and to those who did not.

My story is not a profession of glory or grandeur;

it is about how one person came to realize that it is not what

happens to us but how we react that matters.

Some names and identifying details of people in this book have been changed in order to protect their privacy, but their awesome actions and stories are real.

CRAIG & FRED

CHAPTER 1

Can't Help but Wonder

Summer in North Carolina is the kind of hot you can taste. The air is so humid, it gets caught in your throat, thick like smoke.

Thankfully, with the windows down in the Land Cruiser, I could feel the air beginning to cool, slowly at first, then all at once. I leaned toward the open window, my left arm resting on the doorframe and my right hand on the wheel. The green-blue Smoky Mountains rose up ahead of us and on either side. I took a deep breath and smiled.

In the passenger seat beside me, Josh fiddled with the music till he landed on Johnny Cash. Like the A/C, the radio didn't work, but we'd duct-taped a little Bluetooth speaker to the dash, and it did the trick. Cash sang out the lyrics to "Can't Help but Wonder Where I'm Bound," and we sang along, too, lowering our voices till we broke out laughing.

From the back, Fred popped up his head between us. His mouth was open in a slight pant, and it made him look like he was smiling. "You like the music, buddy?" I asked, and Josh turned to give him a scratch behind his floppy white ear. Fred let out a long, dramatic yawn, complete with a little whine, then curled up again on his nest of blankets and pillows. He had the best seat in the house.

It was the summer of 2015 and we were driving toward the afternoon sun, headed across the country on what we guessed would be a five-week road trip. Our plan, if you could call it one, was loose: drive west till we met the ocean, then north till we hit Seattle, then back east till we were home again. Josh had lobbied for his role as copilot on the trip: "You'll get twice as far for half the cost," he'd insisted. It was an easy decision to bring him. I knew if I went out on the road alone, I'd end up in uselessly challenging situations, pushing myself, the truck, and Fred too hard. Josh, a buddy of mine from Georgetown, was a voice of reason. And, like me, he had been to Afghanistan and back, but neither of us had seen much of our own country.

So we packed up my truck with camping gear—tents, sleeping mats, charcoal, a Ka-Bar knife, plus a football, a Frisbee, and two mountain bikes on the roof rack—and hit the road. The bikes were both mine; I was hoping Josh would be able to bike with me, but I hadn't asked yet. In 2009, Josh lost his leg in Afghanistan when the Stryker his team was driving—an eight-wheeled armored infantry vehicle—struck an IED. The blast destroyed the vehicle and took Josh's right leg from just above the knee down.

He had a pretty badass prosthetic now, complete with a robotic knee, but he hadn't really had the opportunity to put it to the test yet. Recovering from an injury like that isn't exactly a cakewalk, no pun intended. Josh's recovery had entailed a long series of surgeries (the latest just a few months before) on his "good leg," which had also been seriously injured in the blast. Even though he'd graduated from Georgetown the year before our trip, the operations had kept him from getting a job, essentially putting his life on hold. When I'd spotted him at our favorite pub in D.C. a few weeks earlier, he'd looked pretty rough. Josh was a lot taller than me, but he looked as if he'd shrunk. That night, we hastily put the plan together. Within a week, we were off.

It was good timing for me, too. I was still in school full-time at Georgetown but decided to take the summer off. I guess you could say I wanted to soak up my last college summer before graduating and getting back to the grind. A year earlier, I'd bought my dream car—a 1988 Toyota Land Cruiser—after spotting her in a mechanic's lot by my apartment, still wearing her original royal blue paint. Like a lovesick teenager, I kept my eye on the truck for weeks. I was broke, and I didn't even know if it was for sale or not. But when I woke up one morning to find a deposit from the VA in my bank account—a year's worth of disability back pay that suddenly came through—I knew it was time to find out. That same afternoon, I drove her off the lot. Fred assumed his position in the passenger seat, his front paws on the armrest and his head out the window. He stuck his snout high in the air like he always did, as if proud of his new wheels. Ever since, I'd been dreaming of taking him across the country in that truck.

"We're gonna bushwhack," I'd told Josh as we planned our trip. I didn't want to stick to the well-worn trails; we were going to make our own.

"I've got a three-day limit, man," Josh had said, pointing to his knee. "That's the lifespan of the battery in this thing." Once it died, he'd be down to one leg, and we'd be screwed.

Josh was twenty-nine years old, a few years younger than me, and from Minnesota. He had an easygoing personality and got along with everyone. But I knew that, like me, Josh wanted to push limits. Before his injury, he'd been in peak physical condition. He was a tall guy—about six foot one—with a lean, athletic build. He could bench two hundred pounds and hike for ten miles with an eighty-pound ruck on his back, no problem. After the IED, all that changed. He had to relearn how to do everything with one leg. Our trip would be his first chance to really see what he could do.

We began to descend into a valley. The road twisted through the mountains, lined on either side by tall, sheltering trees. Their leaves danced in the wake of the Land Cruiser as we whizzed by. From outside, a powerful roar swelled up, like a train pulling into a station. Josh turned down the music so we could hear. As we sank deeper into the valley, we realized it was the sound of a river below. We looked for a place to pull over so we could walk down and get a closer look.

That's what we wanted: the chance to see something new, to encounter the unexpected, to have each day start with that anticipation of the unknown. It'd been four years since I left the Marine Corps. My time in the marines had been a series of ups and downs, but I always felt that what I was doing was relevant. After I got out, I got a desk job where it felt irrelevant whether I even showed up or not. I wasn't challenged. I wasn't really myself. So I went back to school, just to check a box; I thought if I got my degree, then I could go back to work and get a better job. Move up. Find a challenge. But the more time I spent away from that job, the more I realized I didn't want to go back. What I was going to do instead, I didn't know. When things get easy for me, I get uncomfortable. I was always that way growing up, but after my deployment, that feeling only got stronger.

I'd be lying if I said I wasn't searching for the life I led in Afghanistan by coming on this trip. That might sound crazy, but it's real. Every vet I know at one point or another longs for the day-to-day urgency and uncertainty of life in a combat zone. When you don't know what the day's going to bring, when your only goal is to keep yourself and your buddies alive, everything is stunningly simple. Once you get a taste of that, a lot of things you do at home just don't feel the same.

Some people are haunted by what they did and what they saw in Afghanistan. I'm no exception. Some things you can't forget. But some things you don't want to forget, either, like the memory of your friends who didn't come back. The ones you saw die. The way I was starting to see it, maybe refusing to live my life like a vegetable behind a desk was one way to honor that memory—to honor them. Or maybe it was just my way of coping. Maybe on the road I could find out.

Josh spotted a turnoff and I pulled over. As the truck rolled to a stop, Fred picked his head up. He looked at me, asking a question with a twitch of his eyebrows. "You stay here, Freddy," I said. Josh and I got out and found a steep set of stairs going down. We took our time, step by step. At the bottom, the river was beautiful. We watched the white water clamor over rocks and boulders, creating a continuous sound of churning thunder. We stood on the edge for a few minutes and cooled down in the mist.

Having gotten our fill of misty air and river sounds, Josh and I made our way back up the steps. As we neared the road, I stopped in my tracks. There was Fred, standing at the top of the stairs. He must've jumped right out the car window.

"Fred!" I shouted in that low, you're-in-deep-shit voice of a dog owner. "What are you *doing*?" He sunk his head low and scurried toward Josh. He'd never gotten himself out of the truck like that before. It rattled me. What if a car had been coming by when he was standing in the road? I knew what he really wanted, though: to be with us. Fred had a way of keeping his eye on me—and watching out for me. The three of us were a pack now, from here to California and back.

"C'mon, buddy," I said, more softly. I gently pulled Fred to me by the loose scruff around his neck and kissed him on the forehead. "I'm not gonna leave you."

I opened the car door and Fred leapt up onto his seat, then Josh and I climbed in. I turned the key, and Johnny Cash came crooning through the little speaker. We pulled onto the winding road and continued on our way. It was just the beginning.

CHAPTER 2

Looks Like a Fred

"You guys are gonna be standing in your own piss for a few days." That was an analyst's warning to us about Sangin, Afghanistan. In other words, once we landed, we'd be too busy fighting the Taliban to stop for a bathroom break. He was right.

We inserted by helicopter. The guys didn't talk much on the way out. The inside of a CH-53 is like a leaky washing machine—hollow and noisy—so you can't exactly hold a conversation. Instead we sat there, shoulder to shoulder in the dark, waiting. I tried not to think much about what the analyst said. It was better not to have expectations. I wanted to go in with an open mind. Ready.

I felt the engine shift as we started to descend. It was almost midnight. That's when it was safest for the helicopters—and us. I looked down, checked my gear one last time, and turned on my night vision goggles. *Goggles* isn't really the word; the night vision we used was actually a big monocle. You bring it down from your helmet and position it in front of one eye so you have one eye in the night vision and one in the dark. It's disorienting at first. I was so green on my first mission, I couldn't figure out how to work it. The marines around me all pulled theirs down, turned them on, and I sat there fiddling with mine right up until the landing. Even then I couldn't figure it out, so I gave up and didn't use the goggles at all that night. Maybe they thought I was tough for that, or maybe stupid.

My job was in human intelligence—I was an intelligence collector—so my role in the field was to learn as much as I could about the Taliban from villagers. And if we got hold of a Taliban fighter, I was the only one in the unit who could detain and interrogate him. My first mission, just before this one, had been to Trek Nawa, a town on the outskirts of Marjah. There, I'd earned my Combat Action Ribbon, even detained and questioned a Taliban member. Still, what was true in Trek Nawa wouldn't necessarily be true in Sangin. The way we got briefed on it, we knew it was going to be a different fight.

The guys I was heading out with were RECON marines. If my expertise was in communication, theirs was in combat. They were the real deal—an elite force of special ops guys who were tough and experienced. They were like professional athletes, and smart, too. I didn't want them to think I was a soup sandwich, some nerd from intel who wouldn't bring any value to their mission. Before my deployment, I'd trained my ass off, doing two-a-days at the gym. To earn the trust of my teammates, I knew I would need to demonstrate not just that I was physically able to keep up on long nighttime patrols and in gunfights, but also that I brought something to the battlefield that they couldn't provide for themselves.

It was time to touch down. We sat silently in the helicopter, the green glow from our night vision illuminating our faces. We were getting dropped a couple of miles from a compound that had been scouted out by drone in advance. We'd go in and make it our base, spending the rest of the night filling sandbags and preparing for the attack that would likely come at sunup.

In the previous mission, we had a British royal marine with us called Jack. Good guy. He was supposed to come to Sangin with us, but he bowed out. "I'm not going back there," he'd said. He'd been a couple years earlier, when the British had the task of securing it. "It's the kind of place where you turn a corner and there's two Taliban guys standing there. One's got an RPG and the other's got a machine gun, and they're just waiting to light you up," he said. "Place is bonkers."

Sangin had that reputation. The Taliban were bolder there because it was an important location for poppy farming, and the opium trade was a big way the Taliban financed themselves. Plus, coalition forces hadn't committed enough troops there recently, so the Taliban had total control and complete freedom of movement. We were walking onto their turf. We expected them to have a lot of fighters and a lot of firepower. Nothing was off the table: recoilless rifles, rocket-propelled grenades, rockets, mortars, DShK machine guns. When the Taliban controlled an area like this, they also had power over the families in the villages, who had no choice. At the most basic level, that meant the Taliban took what they wanted from whomever they wanted, shutting down the local economy. These villages were extremely poor, so the Taliban were often the only ones who owned anything of much material value, from sneakers to cell phones to the little motorcycles they drove around in. When they needed food, they'd show up at markets and bakeries and take whatever they wanted. If a motorcycle broke down, they'd find the only mechanic in town and take the parts or make him fix their bikes at gunpoint. They ruined weddings, breaking instruments and punishing guests for dancing. They recruited—or just took— young boys.

With a thud, the helicopter set itself down in a cloud of dust, and we stepped out into the night, rifles up. The desert earth was firm under my boots, and a thin layer of silky dust washed over everything like water. I tried not to cough. The rotors whipped up a heavy haze of dirt and lifted back into the sky. There's nothing like the feeling of that hum disappearing into the distance. When it's just you and the guys on the ground, with no machine to protect you or whisk you away, it gets real.

We got moving, single file to avoid IEDs. There was only the sound of our boots scuffing against the dirt and our rucksacks shifting on our backs. With very little light pollution, Afghanistan is supposed to be ideal for stargazing. But I swear the dust in Sangin never fell from the air. Overhead was only a dark, obscured sky, like a smudged impressionist painting.

We walked two, three miles, over rolling hills, heading west. All told, there were three platoons of marines, plus "attachments" like me and the EOD (explosive ordinance disposal) team, as well as members of the Afghan National Army. In total, there were about sixty of us. Our gear and rucksacks were heavy— seventy pounds or more—but this was what we'd trained to do. After a while my heart rate steadied. My body began to get used to the idea of where we were.

When we came up to the compound, we could see waiting in the doorway an elderly man who must have heard us coming.

We only ever established a base in a compound that was already occupied—one that had "a pattern of life." If folks were already living there and hadn't been blown up, that was as good a sign as any that the place wasn't riddled with IEDs.

Ali, the interpreter on the mission, and I walked up to talk to him. Ali had been on the previous mission with me, and we'd gotten close. He was from Afghanistan but had moved to the U.S. years before. Now, he'd returned to help his homeland, and to make a decent living for his wife and newborn kid back in Arizona.

"Arizona, really?" I used to tease him. "You moved from one desert to another."

"My new desert has air-conditioning, my friend," Ali would say, smiling. Ali loved air-conditioning.

We both stepped up and shook the man's hand. This was the part where I had to explain who we were and that we were here to help—and that we would need the man and his family to move to another compound. Compounds in Sangin ranged in size; most included one or more freestanding structures that served different purposes, like for storing rice or to be used as living quarters. Around the perimeter of the buildings were tall mud walls, and extended families shared the space inside, sometimes along with their livestock. Some compounds stood on their own while others shared a perimeter wall with a neighboring compound. Often in Sangin, the families we encountered were nomadic, moving from compound to compound to work as sharecroppers. In this case, the elderly man told us he and his family hadn't been there very long, and he kindly agreed to relocate. He opened the small metal door of the compound to us, and we filed in. Some of us got to work fortifying the walls and rooftops, while others helped the man and his family move a few hundred yards away to a neighboring compound.

The compound was large. Its thick mud walls stood about twelve feet high and stretched about fifty by twenty yards around us. Inside, there were a few basic structures, little twelve-by-eight-feet huts: one in the northwest corner, where we built a rooftop post; one in the middle, which we turned into a makeshift command center; and two others, each of which we fortified into posts, too. We spent the night filling green plastic sandbags, assembly-line style. Using a collapsible shovel, I helped scoop mounds of dust and dirt into the bags, then another guy would carry them over to the marines on the roof, who would hoist them on top of the little clay buildings. The sandbags—which were bulletproof when filled—got stacked in a raised wall around the perimeter so guys could sit safely inside and look out. Down below, we also dug out holes the size of personal pizzas in the walls. We needed a way to see and shoot out. Murder holes, we called them.

It took all night. When the sky began to turn blue again and light stretched across the horizon, I could see the wide, sweeping desert that stretched out to our east. To the west, the compound overlooked Highway 611, and beyond it, the "Green Zone." We called it the Green Zone because that's where the Helmand River flowed, giving way to lush, green farmland. Fields of corn and poppy unfurled on either side of the river, along with an extensive network of irrigation canals. I watched as a thick coat of mist rose up over the canals, then burned away.

The 611 "highway" was actually an IED-riddled dirt road

that ran north to south, its southernmost point the Sangin District center and its northernmost the Kajaki Dam. Like a tourniquet, the highway divided the irrigated land in the Green Zone from the scorched desert where we had established our post.

The Taliban were in the Green Zone. Our mission was to drive them out so that a company of coalition engineers could safely make their way up Highway 611, from the district center to the Kajaki Dam in the north. With the area secured, the road could be cleared of IEDs, allowing much-needed turbine parts to be delivered to the dam. Once functional, the dam would provide enough energy to bring electricity to the entire region.

Sometimes when I try to describe Sangin to people, I say it's like West Virginia. I don't mean to offend any West Virginians, but our own culture's stereotype of the wild and wonderful mountain state is a useful comparison. It's a way to emphasize how remote and rural Sangin is—so much so that even many Afghans refuse to go there. It's tribal land, home to a low population of residents, most of them farmers who live largely without access to formal education or electricity. That's part of what makes the region so susceptible to Taliban abuse and control.

When Third Battalion, Fifth Marines (Three-Five, or Darkhorse, as they were called), had arrived in the district center a few weeks prior to our mission, they'd walked right into a meat grinder. In the first week, they lost ten guys. We were here not only to help clear out the Taliban from around the highway but also to take some pressure off of the Three-Five marines in the south.

My main objective in Sangin was to figure out who was who. Like a tactical anthropologist, I needed to understand the situation on the ground from a villager's perspective. I needed to get to know the locals. What did people call themselves here? Which tribes did they belong to? How did they earn a living? And how were the Taliban affecting their lives? By building relationships, I'd be able to extract critical information from people firsthand. I also wanted to create a database of people's names, tribes, family members, jobs, and locations. That way, when the Marine Corps continued to secure and maintain the area in the future, they'd have a dossier of everyone who lived there.

In the new daylight, two marines took up post on the rooftop position, turning their binoculars toward the fields. Those CH-53s aren't exactly quiet. People knew we were here. If the Taliban hadn't figured out our location yet, they would soon.

From the roof, one of the marines shouted down.

"I've got movement! Northwest!" he said.

I got in front of a murder hole and looked out into the Green Zone. He was right: I could see people emerging from the edge of the fields and crossing into the desert, coming toward us. But as I watched, I saw that the people were moving slowly. They were carrying things—stuff that looked like sacks of rice and bags of belongings. I saw someone pushing a wheelbarrow carrying an old woman and another leading a donkey with blankets and buckets hanging over either side. These weren't Taliban fighters. They were villagers. They were trekking out of the Green Zone, their possessions on their backs. Fleeing.

They kept coming. For two hours, we watched as dozens of

people made their way out of the Green Zone to the dusty cluster of compounds near ours. If they had stayed where they were, we realized, they risked being turned into targets by the Taliban. Fighters could occupy their homes for shelter while they launched attacks on us. It was a well-known Taliban tactic, and a horrific one at that.

I remember how tired they looked, how defeated. It could've been years since troops were on the ground here, sure, but they'd been through this before. Without us here, their lives were about surviving through Taliban occupation. With us here, they had to survive in a combat zone. *What a fucking mess,* I thought. We needed to get this right. I wanted these people to get the peace and freedom they deserved.

The morning sky swelled with light. Only a few hours in, and already the dust was working its way into my hair, skin, and clothes. Everything had the same stale smell. I grabbed a bottle of water and splashed some on my face, then started my favorite ritual: preparing instant coffee. My sister had given me a little Jetboil stove that could heat water in sixty seconds. It was magic.

Across the compound, I saw Top, our leader and master sergeant, doing the same. A twenty-year veteran with a square jaw and bricks for fists, Top rarely uttered more than two words at once.

I lifted the hot cup of coffee to my lips, then heard it: the distinct, overpowering thunder of an attack.

Directly overhead, the sky screamed, *WHOOSH!*

I looked up and saw it: a rocket soaring through the air, followed by another. They sailed by almost slowly, like they were floating. Their paths crisscrossed and I vaguely registered that they must have been launched from different locations. One buzzed off into the distance, missing our compound. The other cracked open into a sharp, deafening explosion at the far end of the compound—within our walls but, thankfully, where no one was. The blast happened before the thing even hit the ground—it was an airburst RPG. It rattled my teeth and rang in my ears.

I looked back over at Top, who was already moving into action. He ran into our makeshift control center, one of the little clay rooms in the center of the compound, to get on the radio. Around me, the guys were putting on their gear. I looked at Dave, one of the EOD guys, who was already suited up with his body armor and helmet. *Shit*, I thought, and grabbed my stuff.

I rushed to the wall and peered out a murder hole. I saw desert and dust. Nothing. Behind me, the west wall—the one facing the Green Zone—was getting all the action. Rifle rounds hit the clay, sending dirt flying. The guys on the roof shouted to each other, calculating where the RPGs had come from and preparing to return fire.

You could also hear their reports over the radio: we were nearly surrounded; Taliban fire was coming from 270 degrees around us. At first, the guys on the roof were taking some machine gun and small arms fire. But then you could hear their voices change as they reported that "some fire" was now "*accurate* fire." We had only two rooftop positions facing the Green Zone, each with two guys, plus a few murder holes down below. All told, that meant we had only about eight guys returning fire on what was easily a few hundred Taliban. The rounds peppered the sandbags with a near continuous *rat-a-tat-tat-tat-tat-tat*. It became too heavy, and the guys had to duck down. You never want to get pinned down like that; it means you can't beat back the enemy. It means it's only going to get worse. Above, the sky was cloudless and blue.

And then: "*Corpsman!*"

I heard the shrill, urgent call come over the radio from the rooftop position nearest the Green Zone.

Corpsman is not a word you want to hear during a gunfight.

From down on the wall, I looked up and could see that it was Aaron, Joe's watch partner, who was calling out. I knew Joe and Aaron from my first mission; Joe and I had become fast friends when we connected over our shared interest in mountain biking and snowboarding. Now, up on the post, Joe lay limp beside his teammate. *Fuck,* I thought.

Frantically, Aaron unbuckled Joe's helmet while rounds continued to whiz overhead. He grabbed the front lip and tugged, pulling it off so he could get a better look at the injury, try to stop the bleeding.

But Joe's helmet was empty. No blood, no pieces of skull. Aaron looked back at Joe's head, then again at the helmet, trying to reconcile what was going on. He knew Joe had been shot—he was lying there unconscious—but physically, he looked okay. Aaron checked the helmet again and found them: two bullet holes where the round had gone in and then out. Joe groaned and started to move.

"We need to get you down, man," Aaron said. Joe, disoriented, opened his eyes and started to crawl toward the ladder, head first. From below, Jim, the corpsman, slowed him down.

"Hey, hey, hey! Easy, buddy! You gotta turn around!" he shouted up. Dizzy and confused, Joe turned and backed down feet first.

I ran over to the bottom of the ladder and waited with Jim. We eased Joe down and propped him up in the dirt. Jim started to examine Joe's head, parting his short hair with his fingers. Meanwhile, Aaron continued returning fire overhead.

There was no wound to be found. Joe—somehow—was okay. The round had skimmed through the top of his helmet without hitting his head at all.

The first attack didn't last long—less than a half hour—but it felt like forever. One minute hell's breaking loose around you, the next minute it gets quiet. You realize you're soaked in sweat, you're wearing all this heavy armor and a helmet in one-hundred-degree heat, and your mouth is an oven. But you're alive.

Within an hour, the next attack came. It was similar to the first. The Taliban liked to start with something dynamic— using a big, powerful weapon, hoping to inflict casualties. Sometimes that meant an RPG or mortar fire; sometimes it was heavy fire from a large-caliber rifle at close range, like a DShK (pronounced "dishka"). It could also be a recoilless rifle, a type of lightweight tube artillery, fired from a truck or from the ground. They always launched attacks from at least two locations, followed by mortars and gunfire. Then they'd recover and reposition, launching the next attack about an hour later. It would continue like this until sundown.

We had days on end of this. The guys took shifts on the roofs. The rounds came in. The temperature rose. We took fire;

we returned it. For a short span of time in the afternoons, when the sun rose high in the sky and it got to be 115 degrees Fahrenheit, the desert fell quiet. It was unbearable to do anything, and for a couple of hours, the Taliban stopped their assault.

We spent the time cleaning our guns and eating our MREs ("meals ready to eat," aka vacuum-sealed military-issue space food). We played cards and took naps. We tried to make jokes, cool down, clean off. We were already filthy, covered in dirt freckles—little specks of dust on our skin no baby wipe could get off. Our "bathroom" was a chicken coop where we did our business in little silver bags with deodorizing powder, then tossed them in a burn pit. In less time than you might think, all of it kind of becomes a new normal.

It was between Taliban attacks that I spotted him.

I was hot and exhausted, trying to stay cool in sandals and the thin green running shorts we called "silkies." I stood refilling my water bottle and heating some water for Ali, who, despite the heat, insisted on a cup of tea with his lunch. As I put the cap on my water bottle, I watched a goofy-looking dog trot across the compound. With his short legs and puppylike pep, he looked nothing like other stray dogs I'd seen in Afghanistan. Most were tall and bulky, and they moved around in packs, aggressive over territory and scavenged food.

I could tell this dog was different. He didn't have a pack; he was alone. He pranced nonchalantly in the dust, tail bobbing and snout held high, as if he was particularly proud of the morsel of food he was carrying. There was something innocent about him; he seemed unaffected by life in a combat zone.

I'd noticed his routine before in the day or so since we'd been in the compound. The dog would go over to the burn pit to rummage for something to eat, then carry little scraps back to his makeshift den, which was a shady spot under a few bushes. *Funny little hoarder,* I thought.

When we first arrived at the compound, I asked the old man about a couple of dogs that were hanging around. "Are they yours?" I asked. If so, we'd help transport them to the family's new compound, along with the livestock.

"No, no, no," he told us. It would have been unusual for a farmer in Sangin to have a pet dog. The villagers loved animals and took great care of their livestock, but they were focused on surviving and on feeding their families; they couldn't afford to feed and care for a pet. Occasionally, when we did come across "pet" dogs, they were actually used for fighting.

After the family left and we moved in, the little dog stayed. It was almost as if this were his compound. I stood and watched him flop down in his spot under the bushes. Beside him I could see other food scraps he'd accumulated: little MRE wrappers, sticks, bones.

I put down my water bottle, picked up a piece of beef jerky, and started walking over to him, my sandaled feet kicking up dust. When the dog realized I was coming his way, he stopped eating and looked at me. He watched as I approached, squinting to shield his eyes from the dust and sun.

A few steps away from him, I paused.

"Hey, buddy," I said. "How's it going?"

He seemed to be studying me. There was something expressive about his big, light brown eyes—almost humanlike. For a moment, we just looked at each other. Then I heard a quiet *thwap thwap thwap*. A little cloud of dust kicked up into the air behind him. I couldn't believe it: he was wagging his tail.

I took it as an invitation to move closer and crouched down to get a better look at him. The dog's fur was mostly white, with large spots of light orange-brown. He had a long snout with a big black nose and floppy ears. As he looked at me, his eyebrows twitched from side to side, curious. He continued to wag his tail, and his expression was soft and easy, as if he was smiling.

The dog seemed happy as a clam, but I could see he was covered in black bugs the size of dimes. They were buzzing around him, then burrowing into the fur on his face and neck.

I extended my arm, holding out the piece of beef jerky. "Here you go, buddy," I said.

The dog stood up and shook, as if to rid himself of as many bugs as possible before getting near me. He took a few steps forward, his nose leading the way, and inspected my offering before carefully pulling it from my hand with his front teeth. I laughed watching him chew the jerky. Most dogs I knew didn't bother chewing treats before sending them down the hatch.

"Well, you've got better manners than most, don't you?" I said, and extended my other hand so he could give it a few sniffs. With his permission, I massaged my fingers into the fur around his neck and under his ears. It was coarse and matted in dust; it felt unnaturally stiff, almost like a dirty pair of jeans. But the dog happily leaned into me, pleased with the neck rub. I wondered if it was the first time he'd ever been petted.

I'd always wanted a dog as a kid. I even went so far as to buy a leash with my own money, then went around knocking on our neighbors' doors after school, volunteering to walk their dogs for free. Some of them actually let me. My favorite dog was an old basset hound named Irene. She had these big paws and enormous floppy ears. When I walked her, she'd trot ahead of me, out at the end of the leash, with her snout high in the air, taking in all the smells she could. This dusty pup with his long body and short legs made me think of her.

Before I got carried away with him, though, I stopped myself. Cozying up to dogs was off-limits in Afghanistan. When I first arrived in-country, back at the main base, I'd sat through two full days of orientation where they laid out all the rules, big and small. No alcohol. No porn. No saluting superiors, for tactical reasons. One of the memorable ones came from a veterinarian from the military police K-9 unit. "No dogs," she said plainly, then proceeded to tell us horror stories about guys contracting rabies. Get caught with a stray dog, she said, and that dog will be euthanized, no questions asked. On top of that, I was still hyperfocused on proving myself to the RECON guys. I had to show my worth on this mission, not sit around in the dust with a dog.

With that in mind, I reluctantly got up. The dog just stood there, gazing up at me. "Okay, buddy," I said. I turned and headed back toward my corner of the compound.

But after taking just a few steps, I felt a little nudge at the back of my ankle. I looked down to see the dog staring up at me with a toothy grin, tail wagging again. From across the compound, Matt, one of the EOD guys, had been watching our exchange. "Looks like you made a friend!" he shouted. But what I heard was, "Looks like a *Fred*!" The name stuck.

Fred trotted along behind me back to the makeshift campsite

where I had my sleeping mat. I didn't try to stop him. Maybe there wasn't that much harm in giving him another piece of jerky and some water, I thought.

I grabbed a large tin bowl that was lying around—it had probably been for the cows—and filled it with water from my canteen. Placing it down in front of Fred, I watched as he licked the thing dry. I stood over him and smiled. Just as he'd taken the jerky from me with a gentle tug, he drank water the same way, with polite little laps.

Jim, the corpsman, had been watching, too. You got the feeling Jim had been an Eagle Scout as a kid. He was super bright and always had any tools he needed close by. He got up from his spot in the shade and came over, taking a closer look at the bugs on Fred's neck. He pulled out a set of tweezers from his fanny pack and, pointing to the bugs, said, "Why don't you hold him steady, and we'll see if I can get some of these bloodsuckers off?"

The two of us crouched down in the dirt. I sat cross-legged and pulled Fred toward me, holding him by the shoulders. The bugs, like flying ticks, were digging into Fred's fur and attaching to his hide. Getting them out meant Jim was going to have to pull them from his skin.

"Careful, dude," I said, as Jim narrowed in on one, closing down on it with the tweezers. I didn't know how Fred was going to react. In one quick motion, Jim yanked hard and, between the prongs of the tweezers, pulled away the first bug, along with a clump of Fred's fur. I braced myself for a yowl or nip from Fred, but he just sat there, unbothered. Jim and I exchanged looks. Carefully, he kept going, pulling out one bug at a time. Patiently, Fred just sat there, letting us do our work.

When we finished, a tiny bug graveyard had piled up in the dirt beside us. Jim gave Fred a pat on the top of the head and stood up. "Wow," he said. "I can't believe he let us do that."

Fred, in his newfound freedom, shook again, then walked to my sleeping mat. He stepped over the edge of the bug net—a single-person cocoon-like shelter we each slept inside—and climbed in, pawing at the material to arrange it how he wanted. It was as if he'd done it a hundred times before. Content with the arrangement, he lay down, let out a sigh, and blinked his eyes closed. I was caked in dirt, too, and I didn't mind at all if the dusty pup wanted a spot on my bed. Jim and I laughed.

"Little guy is making himself right at home!" he said.

I leaned over and zipped up the bug net for our new friend. I was some six thousand miles from home, in a combat zone, in one of the harshest places in the world. And here was this dog. Unlike me, Fred *was* home. Sangin was all he knew. And even though he'd probably never had a drink of clean water before or a scratch behind the ear, he was gentle and sweet. Looking down at him, I stopped worrying about the no-dog policy or when the next RPG would pierce the sky. For that moment, I felt like I was home, too.

CHAPTER 3

School's Out

Back in the truck, Josh and I wound our way through the mountains, edging closer to our first destination: Chattanooga, Tennessee. In the backseat, Fred snored peacefully.

Josh and I had first met a year earlier, in my very first class at Georgetown. "Modern Borders," it was called, a political science course about how countries were shaped throughout history. I'd walked into the room just before class started and spotted a tall guy in the back with a beard like mine and a prosthetic leg. His backpack lay on the floor next to him and a dirty Nalgene bottle sat on his desk. I went straight for him.

Plopping myself down in the desk next to Josh, I said, "Hey, man. Isn't it a little cold out for shorts?"

"I like feeling the cool air on my leg," he quipped. I knew we'd be friends.

Later, Josh told me he knew I was a marine by the way I carried myself. I told him I knew he was army from the patches on his backpack. Army guys love their patches.

Before enrolling at Georgetown, I never really pictured myself as a college student. And after spending eight years in the marines, going back to school wasn't at the top of my priority list. As a kid, I'd never been much of a student. I knew I was smart, and I loved school, but it was hard for me to learn in a classroom. My attention span was short and my energy was high. I never understood why we were supposed to sit still for so long. In elementary school, I was diagnosed with ADD. I started medication, but it made me miserable and gave me insomnia.

I was normally upbeat and boisterous, so my friends didn't know what was wrong with me when I started showing up at school every day with a blank look on my face, tired and deflated. When my mom gave me the pill every morning, I started hiding it under my tongue, then spitting it out on the walk to the bus stop.

One day during my sophomore year of high school, recruiters from all five military branches came to our school. A representative from the navy stood up, clicking through a PowerPoint presentation on a projector behind him, explaining to the full auditorium what it meant to join the navy and all the benefits of doing so. A guy from the air force did the same thing, and the army. When the Marine Corps rep took the stage, the screen behind him went blank. He didn't have a slide show or a presentation. He stared out into the faces of the kids in front of him, gripping the podium as if he were about to lift it overhead. Then he said one thing: "Maybe three or four of you have what it takes to be a marine. If you think you're one of them, come talk to me." With that, he stepped down. I didn't have the nerve to talk to him that day, but it left an impression on me.

Growing up outside Washington, D.C., it wasn't unusual to know people who had served in the military. Our neighborhood might as well have been base housing for the Pentagon. My dad had been in the air force during the Vietnam era and served as an investigator for the National Transportation Safety Board after getting his degree on the G.I. Bill. By my senior year of high school, I started thinking seriously about joining the marines. My friends were all applying to go to college, but I couldn't imagine facing another four years of school.

Then my parents split. It was one of those things that, as a kid, just kind of sneaks up on you. After my big sister, Sarah, went away to college, it was just me and my parents in the house. My mom and dad both traveled a lot for work, so I was used to that. I was also used to my parents sleeping in separate rooms. I thought they just preferred it that way; maybe my dad snored. I didn't think too much about it, maybe because I didn't want to, or didn't know how. I was busy, too; it was my senior year, and I had a lot going on between my travel hockey team and an active social calendar.

I came home from an out-of-town ice hockey tournament, though, and Mom wasn't home. She was on a work trip, I figured, but then I found a note in my room. She'd written it to me, explaining that she and my father were splitting up. It probably shouldn't have come as a surprise—she'd even said something to me about moving to South Carolina—but she hadn't been direct, and I didn't realize she was trying to say good-bye. My dad hadn't said anything. I guess the two of them didn't know how to explain their problems to me, and I was too busy being a seventeen-year-old to have picked up on the signs. I didn't know how to handle it, so I ignored it. I had enough to distract me.

My mom had been the one to take Sarah to visit college campuses her senior year. Now it was just my dad and me at home, and my grades weren't good. I'd brought up the Marine Corps to him, but he didn't want to hear it. He urged me to try community college.

As my high school graduation approached, I was at risk of failing two required classes. Still, no one said anything. Instead, I was nominated by my peers to be the speaker at our senior ceremony. When I failed the classes and showed up on graduation day, I waited for the other shoe to drop. It didn't. I had heard stories about the administration letting students walk at graduation, then, instead of a diploma, those students would get a letter ordering them to summer school. But after I made my speech and was handed a big manila envelope, I was stunned to find a diploma inside.

I acted happy about it, but it didn't feel right to me. Now more than ever, I wanted to be challenged and held accountable, and it seemed like no one was going to do that for me. I daydreamed about how, if I joined the marines, I'd be held to a higher standard. I'd get my ass kicked. To me, it was an organization that recognized hard work and nothing less. I craved that. It was what I loved about playing ice hockey. If you didn't do the work, you didn't get to play. Only the strongest and fastest made the cut—no excuses.

Ultimately, though, I enrolled in community college, promising my dad I'd give it a try.

Then 9/11 happened. Like many future enlistees, I was filled with an overwhelming sense of duty. I wanted a purpose and a mission. This was a clearer sign than any. When my semester was finished at community college, I enlisted. When I came home with my paperwork from the processing center, my dad didn't mince words. "The marines?" he said. "You're gonna be cannon fodder." I knew he was proud I'd joined but also troubled I'd chosen the branch of the military notorious for being at the front lines of war.

Because I'd enlisted in a delayed entry program and because of the high volume of enlistees after the September 11 attacks, it wasn't until March 2003 that I was finally able to report to boot camp in Parris Island, South Carolina. I promptly began receiving the ass-kicking I'd been waiting for. We were shouted at from morning till night, drilled at length on everything from putting on a sock to hitting a target at five hundred yards. There were no comforts. The bathrooms, for instance, had no stalls. You shit in the open, and it's not unusual for a drill instructor to come in and dump water on you—and the toilet paper—while you're at it. It felt like we were nothing more than livestock, and I guess that was the point. By the end of the first phase, I learned how to operate coolly and efficiently under the merciless reign of the drill instructors. I was determined to accomplish every task in spite of their efforts to distract and disrupt. I was becoming a marine.

Toward the end of training, my fellow recruits and I shuffled into a large warehouse where we were issued our dress uniforms. Our measurements were taken by a laser-scanning machine that spit out our sizes onto paper receipts. As I waited in line to receive my issue of starchy green pants and paper-thin khaki shirts, I noticed my receipt read "PFC Grossi," for private first class. That had to be a mistake. I was a private, the lowest enlisted rank, and I hadn't received a promotion to PFC. The only way that could happen in boot camp was if the senior drill instructor meritoriously selected you, but as far as I knew, that hadn't occurred.

I tried in vain to explain to the young supply marine that there was a mistake on my receipt, but I was pretty much told to go fuck myself. The next morning, I put on my "pickle suit," the green dress coat and matching pants, complete with a khaki tie and shirt underneath. My one ribbon was pinned to my chest and the fresh PFC chevrons were burning a hole in my shoulder. Alone in a sea of itchy fabric, I was just waiting for a drill instructor to rip those chevrons right off. Still, no one reacted.

A few days later came the company commander's inspection. We'd be drilled by a high-ranking marine on everything we'd learned over the past three months. We were expected to be able to answer in a moment any question shot our way, from the maximum effective range of an M203 grenade launcher to the sixth general order of a sentry. I had been selected as a squad leader, so I spent most of the morning making sure each of my squad members had a properly tied tie and a good shave. I'd been told by my recruiter and by other marines to avoid becoming a leader while at boot camp. "Just keep your head down and don't volunteer for anything. If you're a squad leader, it just means extra work," they said, but the philosophy never sat right with me. I'd joined the marines because I was tired of flying under the radar.

On inspection day, my platoon was first. I remember the perfectly polished silver oak leaf pinned to the collar of the

company commander inspecting us. That meant he was a lieutenant colonel. My squad and I needed to have our shit tight.

The lieutenant colonel stepped up in front of me, giving me
and my rifle a slow once-over from top to bottom.

"What did you do to receive your promotion, PFC Grossi?"
he said.

I froze. I still had no idea.

"Sir, this recruit does not know why he was promoted, sir," I
said, unable to come up with anything better to say. The lieutenant colonel looked back at my drill instructors over his right
shoulder. Two of them shot me a gaze that made me want to
shit my pants. The senior drill instructor grinned and shook his
head, then the lieutenant colonel looked at me and said, "Well,
I think you're gonna find out."

My senior drill instructor walked over to me. He was a big
guy with dark skin. I could see the veins in his arms curl like
little blue pipes around his tattoos. He had been a father figure
to me and my fellow recruits—firm but fair.

"I never told you why I promoted you, Grossi?" he said.

"No, sir," I replied.

"I've been watching you. I see what you do for your platoon
when nobody is watching. That's what's most important: doing
the right thing with no anticipation of reward," he said.

All the discipline in the world couldn't hold back the tears
that rolled down my cheeks. In that moment, I felt like I was
exactly where I was supposed to be. It wasn't about the promotion; it was the fact that I finally felt seen. I was good at
something, and my hard work was recognized.

My pride was promptly checked. The other two drill instruc-

tors reminded me that I had botched my answer to the lieutenant colonel and that I was crying like a bitch in my uniform. I
paid for it in the sand pit that night, but I did so with pleasure.
I had found my place. All the push-ups and mountain climbers
in the world couldn't extinguish the fire inside me.

Despite my promising start in the Marine Corps, the years
that followed boot camp were a massive letdown. I had joined
to be a military police (MP) officer, because I had always been
interested in law enforcement and I thought doing it in the
marines would be a great way to serve my country. Later, it
could potentially lead to a career as a cop. I'd also heard that
MPs could be selected to attend K-9 training. I loved dogs and
really loved the idea of being able to work with one every day.

However, I learned a hard lesson about the marines after
boot camp: it didn't matter what you wanted to do; it all
boiled down to the needs of the corps. I ended up working
in corrections, a field I had little interest in, and was assigned
as a guard in Camp Delta (Guantanamo Bay) and then a
naval brig in Charleston, South Carolina, that contained U.S.
servicemen confined for everything from being late to work
to murder, rape, and drug trafficking. I made the most of my
time but never really felt that I was properly challenged. While
my fellow marines were invading Fallujah and Ramadi, I was
scooping chow for detainees in Gitmo, who occasionally liked
to throw their bodily fluids in my face. It was not the duty I
had signed up for.

In 2007, I completed my four years of active service, never

leaving the corrections field. My command refused to let me retrain into another, more deployable field. Feeling frustrated and emasculated, I returned home to northern Virginia. For nine months, I drifted aimlessly from job to job with no real purpose. I knew I could be recalled at any time, and if that happened, I'd likely get put back in corrections. I didn't want to end up at another brig, and I didn't want to sit around at home, either. I decided to reenlist.

I remember how annoyed my recruiter was when I said I didn't want to go back to corrections and told him I didn't want to try a regular military police unit, either, which he kept advocating.

"All right, hotshot. What do you want to do, then?" he asked.

The truth was, I wanted to be in special operations. I was still seeking what I had been from the beginning: I wanted to be pushed and challenged. I wanted to work hard for a team that demanded the best of me. So, I told him I wanted to be a RECON marine. The recruiter scoffed. Being in special ops is what everyone thinks they want, so when you say RECON, they automatically think you're just another wannabe tough guy.

"Listen," he said. "I can't help you with RECON, but you should talk to the guys downstairs. You might be interested in what they do—they have a lot of medals on their chests. They do their own recruiting, so I can't make any promises, but I can put your name in."

That was my introduction to the Marine Corps intelligence field. I knew it was the right fit on my first appointment.

I showed up in a suit. I wasn't on active duty and wasn't sure if it was okay to wear my uniform. The building was on a naval installation near Virginia Beach. It wasn't anything special—just a two-story cinder-block office building with a flagpole out front. When I knocked on the door, a short, muscled staff sergeant opened it a crack and looked at me.

"Put these on," he said, abruptly extending a pair of handcuffs.

I looked down at the shiny metal restraints. Before accepting them, without thinking, I said, "Why?"

With that, he yanked the door open. Two larger marines stood on the other side of the frame. They reached through the doorway, grabbed me by the collar, and pulled me inside.

Asking that question—*Why?*—was what literally got me through the door. It was a test. As a marine, you learn to do what you're told, with a "Yes, sir." But intelligence needed marines who could also think for themselves. I found out later that anyone who put on the handcuffs without hesitation got the door slammed in their face.

When we were growing up, my friends told me more than once that I was a good listener. It never crossed my mind that that quality would translate into a job skill until I ended up in intelligence. In training, I learned how to question, screen, collect evidence, and interrogate. I practiced meeting with a source whose role was to act scared and reticent, and I'd carefully extract information from them through conversation. I realized being a good intelligence collector meant being able to listen and to form relationships with people in all kinds of situations. I was a natural.

Only after six months of on-the-job training would the intel team decide whether it was worth sending me through another four months of classroom training. Seats in class had to be earned. They wanted to make sure you had a decent shot at making it through the rigorous course before they gave you one. The six months flew by, and when I found out I'd been selected to continue training, I was thrilled. Over the following four months, I was challenged in ways I never could have predicted. There were intense, immersive, scenario-based training sessions combined with rigorous academic courses in everything from human behavior to report writing. We had an exam at the end of every week, and any score less than 80 percent was considered a failure. There were many moments when I thought I'd be dropped from the course. While I'd grown up thinking I wasn't "book smart," I realized I could succeed in a classroom environment when I enjoyed the material and found it relevant and interesting. I'd found a challenge worth attempting. I slowly overcame my fear of the academic setting and my confidence began to grow. The class started with thirty candidates; by the end, there were fifteen of us. I'd made it.

Then, about a year later, I finally got the orders I'd been waiting for: we were going to Afghanistan.

CHAPTER 4

Sergeant Fred

Fred quickly became popular in the compound. Within forty-eight hours, the guys started calling him Freddy or Freddy Zone, a combination of his name and combat zone. "Hey, Freddy Zone!" we'd call out in the stretches of afternoon when the compound was hot and quiet. Fred would mosey over for a pet and a treat, happy for the attention.

I started to share my MREs with him here and there. One day I smeared peanut butter on the roof of his mouth, and he sat there smacking his lips, trying to reach every last bit with his tongue while I giggled. He was like a little brother.

One of the guys found a piece of rope and started using it to play tug-of-war with Fred, getting him all riled up. He started to get vocal, barking and howling with excitement. Sometimes he'd bare his teeth, too, which cracked us up. He'd flash his big white grin, growling to try to seem fierce, but with his funny short legs and sweet personality, we didn't buy it.

Our favorite topic of conversation was Fred's goofy looks. Not only was he much smaller than any other dogs we came across in Afghanistan—no more than thirty pounds—but his short legs were an anomaly we loved. Being low to the ground didn't hurt Fred's pride. He always trotted around the compound like a show dog, head up, tail bouncing, paws flicking the dirt. He had an irresistible combination of innocence and confidence.

After Joe was shot that first day, he spent nearly a week holed up in a little room in the compound that had been designated as an aid station. Joe was okay—the bullet hadn't pierced his skull—but the impact of the shot gave him a hellish concussion. He needed to be medevaced out. In the meantime, the doc kept him in the cool, dark room so he could rest. Nauseated and with the worst headache of his life, Joe lay on a mat in pain, in and out of sleep, waiting. At the same time Joe was injured, the Three-Five marines were getting ambushed by the Taliban in their position. They were losing guys and needed support. As a result, Joe had to wait days for a medevac.

On the first day, Fred showed up in the doorway to the aid station. He paused and looked at Joe, then walked up. Leaning in with his hot breath, Fred sniffed Joe's face, pressing his wet nose into his cheek. Then he lay down next to him, resting his head right across Joe's chest. Fred let out a sigh and looked up, meeting Joe's eyes, as if asking, "You okay?" Slowly Fred closed his eyes and just lay there with Joe. Then, after a few minutes, just like that, he got up and left. A couple of hours later, though, Fred came back. He went through the same routine of lying for a few minutes with Joe, checking on him, then leaving. He kept at it for days, monitoring Joe until his medevac came. It was clear there was something remarkable about this dog.

During firefights, none of us could afford to get distracted with Fred's whereabouts. We assumed he had a way of taking care of himself. Once, though, the Taliban were unusually effective during an attack, landing a mortar round just outside the perimeter wall of our compound. It felt like the earth was about to split open. Our mortar team and spotters remained posted while the rest of us took cover in the command center. We huddled together, waiting. Then, through the open doorway, I spotted Fred. He was grazing through the burn pit looking for scraps like he always did. His nose was to the ground as he nudged through dirt like a lazy detective looking for clues.

The guys and I looked at each other, all with the same mental image: a well-placed round landing on our new friend, sending him into the air in bits and pieces.

"Fred!" we shouted. "*Fred!*"

The dog continued to nose through the garbage.

"Hey, shithead! Get the fuck in here!"

Finally, Fred looked up at us. He blinked in the sun, looking mildly confused, then promptly put his nose back to the earth and continued foraging.

Overhead, one of our spotters on the rooftop post yelled, "Incoming!" and we braced for impact. This time, the round landed at the far end of the compound, sending a bone-rattling shock wave throughout the place. That got Fred's attention. He took off, kicking up a cloud of dust as he went, darting right into our shelter and wiggling his way to safety between our legs.

In those early days, while Fred was becoming part of the team, I still worried if befriending the dog might be putting him at risk. If the command perceived him to be a distraction or threat in any way, he'd be cooked.

In the compound, I kept my eye on Top, the command master sergeant, who I saw watching us play with Fred. Top was a huge, silent marine who I'd probably only ever exchanged about four words with. One night, on the previous mission, I'd helped him carry his rucksack across a canal during a patrol. I was standing hip-deep in water, in the middle of the canal, so the guys could pass me their rucks, then leap across. Top walked up and looked at me. Holding out his pack, he said, "It might be heavy," then dropped it into my arms. The weight of the thing sunk me and my boots four inches into the mud. It must have been ninety pounds, almost twice as heavy as the others, full of radio gear and two weeks' worth of backup batteries the size of bricks. I thought it was going to crush me like a paperweight before a teammate on the other side helped take it from me. Then Top leapt across the canal, picked it up, and flung it across his back like it was a lunch box.

He was that strong. I swear we never saw him eat or sleep. Top had been in the corps since the nineties, deploying twice to Iraq and once to Somalia. He was a real leader, and we all respected him. I knew he'd do what he needed to in order to keep us safe. That included making sure a stray dog didn't compromise what we were here to do.

I had all this on my mind one afternoon as I sat in the shade, eating the last bites of my lunch. Fred was shuffling around, sniffing our stuff, and I watched him drift about, looking like he was after a shady spot to settle down in. Across the compound, Top leaned in the doorway of the command center, finishing off his MRE. Fred started to walk toward Top, panting slightly in the heat. The bugs had left him alone since we'd plucked them away, but his fur was still caked in dust. Some of it poofed off his back as he walked.

Fred got to where Top was standing and looked up. They met eyes for a minute, then Fred dropped his hind legs and sat down next to the big marine. The two of them gazed across the compound in the same direction, almost like they were chewing on the same thought. I wondered how this was going to play out. Before then, I hadn't seen Fred and Top interact with each other.

Top scooped one last bite of whatever he was eating into his mouth, then squatted next to Fred. He put the plastic MRE container in front of Fred's mouth, as if to say, "Here." Then Fred leaned in, wiggled his nose, and started licking up the last bit of Top's meal. Top wore sunglasses, so it was hard to make out his expression, but I thought I saw a hint of a smile.

Atta boy, I thought. Fred was making friends in high places.

In Sangin, the RECON marines were discretionary shooters. That meant they had the authority and responsibility to decide when to shoot first. Most of them were higher ranking and had been in the military for years. They could handle those rules of engagement, which not only sent a message to the Taliban that we were serious, but ensured that we didn't get overrun in an area where the Taliban had total control.

As a result, after those first few days, the fighting became less frequent. There was talk of starting night patrols into the Green Zone. We could scout out the area, talk to any villagers who were still over there, and try to get a better idea of what was going on. It was time for me to do my job.

Twelve of us would go out on a carefully premapped route.

The first cluster of compounds we planned to approach was only about a mile away, but our route there would be three. Taking roads, paths, and bridges was out of the question. There was almost certainly a network of IEDs encircling us, as well as ones planted along walkways. Instead, we'd cut through fields and wade through canals, moving in a single file and creating our own path. And we wouldn't return on the same route we took out. Meanwhile, Top would stay near the radio to receive status updates as we went. We'd leave in the dark and be back before the sun came up, staying out no more than eight hours.

As the sun set, the twelve of us lined up our kits along the wall—body armor, helmets, bandoliers, magazines, night vision. I added a notepad and a small, battery-powered camera to my pile. We'd only been in the compound a few days, but it had become our safe haven. Leaving it to walk straight into Taliban territory made my stomach churn.

I took a seat on an ammo crate and ate dinner: a spaghetti MRE. It was my favorite among the other choices of beef stroganoff, chili mac, and chicken and rice. My paternal grandparents were Italian, and I used to smile thinking about how Nonie and Pop-pop would have shaken their heads at these limp noodles and condensed sauce. Beside me, Ali drank chai and used my satellite phone to make a quick call to his family. I wasn't supposed to let anyone use my phone, but it was worth it to bend the rules for Ali, who had a family back home.

When Ali wrapped up his call, he pointed toward my gear and smiled. "Fred's keeping track of you," he said.

I looked up. Fred had made a bed out of my stuff, curling up right on my flak vest.

"He's your boss," Ali said with a laugh.

I smiled. "He wants to know when I leave so he can jump into my sleeping bag," I said. Secretly, I wondered if the dog was getting attached to me. Fred was winning over all the marines one by one, but I felt like we had a special connection.

The sun disappeared on the horizon in an orange blaze. After a few hours, when the sky was black, we lined up at the wall and started suiting up. Fred had gone off somewhere, and I tried to stay focused. Top stood by the tiny tin door that opened in the direction of the Green Zone. One by one, we ducked through and stepped out, Top counting us as we went.

The night was cool and quiet. Through my night vision, the desert looked like the surface of the moon cast in shades of green. Each time my boot hit the ground, a little *poof* of dust erupted around it. The looseness of the dirt made it easy for the Taliban to plant IEDs. I looked ahead to the guy in front of me, then glanced down to watch where I was stepping, then scanned the horizon and checked my flanks through the night vision. Pashto phrases ran through my head. I thought about how I'd introduce myself to villagers and the questions I'd ask.

At the edge of the desert, we came to a ridge that overlooked the lush fields below. I could feel the change in climate. The air was moist and dank, and I thought I could make out the sound of water flowing below. As we walked along the ridge, I suddenly caught a glimpse of something moving off my left flank. Instinctively, I turned, gripping my rifle. But what I saw wasn't a person.

Dumbfounded, I realized it was Fred. There he was, scampering along the way he always did, with light feet, head held high. His tail bobbed up and down. He had the air of a tour guide showing a group of visitors around his turf, even though none of us had ever seen him leave the compound. The other guys had noticed him, too, and we all just smiled in disbelief.

This dog's full of surprises, I thought.

At the planned location, two marines made their way down the ridge. There was a canal at the bottom that looked pretty wide, and they'd evaluate how to best cross it. The rest of us formed a protective circle, took a knee, and scanned the horizon. Fred, who until then had kept his distance, came up and nudged me on the hip. I gave him a quick scratch behind the ear, feeling the familiar dingy fur on his warm neck, and then watched as he went up to the next guy. He moved along quietly, offering nudges and receiving pets. Our little field dog was herding his marines.

The guys at the bottom of the ridge radioed for us to follow. We were officially crossing into the Green Zone. I drew a deep breath.

We filed down the steep cliff and prepared to cross the canal. One at a time, we slid down a muddy bank and waded through. The water was cold and deep; it came up to my waist. I held my rifle overhead and put my notebook in my mouth. The mud on the bed of the canal suctioned the soles of my boots with each step, so I tried to move quickly to keep from sinking. At the opposite side, the guys pulled me out, then I waited to help the next guy. As I turned around, I looked back to see that Fred was in the canal, swimming across to us. His snout and tail were high above the water, and I could see the effort of his little legs paddling along. *No fucking way,* I thought. He really doesn't want to miss out on anything.

The terrain in the Green Zone was immediately different from the desert. The ground was muddy and damp, and on the horizon, corn and poppy fields shimmered in the moonlight. The only sound was of our boots slapping the mud.

We made our way past a small village with a few abandoned compounds. A pack of dogs began howling and moaning when we walked by. They were big, much bigger than Fred, and their sharp barks rattled off the walls of the compounds behind them. A few came close to our patrol, their heads hung low and their fur raised in ridges along their backs. They looked like wolves mixed with hyenas. We moved quickly so that they'd quiet. I looked around for Fred, anxious that he'd start barking or that he'd somehow instigate the pack. I glanced behind me and there he was, moving along quickly at my heel in silence, head down, eyes ahead. Later, when the guys and I talked back at the compound, it was that moment—on top of everything else—that truly blew us away. It was as if Fred knew how to be a marine. He had ignored any instinct he might have had to bark back at the pack of dogs. We were quiet, so he was, too.

We made our way through, carefully crossing three more canals, until finally we reached our destination village. I was soaked and muddy, and the night was cold, but my nerves and our trek kept my blood warm. It was time for Ali and me to get to work.

The first compound had a big green metal door. It was too risky to walk right up to it and knock. The marines covered our position, looking out, as I tossed clumps of dirt at the door. The metal vibrated in response, creating a high-pitched sound. Ali called out in Pashto that we wanted to talk.

The door opened, and an older man in a white robe leaned out. Ali spoke to him, quickly and quietly explaining who we were and asking if we could talk. Because he was so receptive, Ali asked if he could gather some of his neighbors so we could have a *shura,* a meeting typically conducted between village elders. He stepped out from behind the door and together we walked to the next compound, then another, recruiting a few neighbors. One of them rolled out a blanket in a nearby field, and we sat to talk. The RECON guys fanned out wide, almost out of sight, standing post. Fred walked around at a distance, sniffing the ground and looking out.

The conversation was brief. The men were kind and answered our routine questions about what tribe they were part of, their ages, and their names. They didn't have much to say about the Taliban, which we respected. It was possible that they really didn't have any information, or maybe they didn't want to get involved. I took pictures of each person for my report, and we thanked them for gathering with us.

We went to one more village before making our way back, taking a long, circuitous route to the compound. The terrain in the Green Zone was complex and exhausting, but we were safe. As we ducked through the doorway, Top stood waiting as he had been when we left. He greeted us each by name. "Well done, Craig," he said to me. Fred, who had stayed with us for the entire journey, scampered through. Smiling, Top said, "Well done, Sergeant Fred."

We assembled in Top's command center to compare notes. I took a seat in the back on a bag of rice. The red glow of a lantern lit up our tired, mud-smudged faces, and the green glimmer of the command radio flickered in the corner. Top looked around and counted heads. Someone joked, "Where's Fred?" As if on cue, he came trotting into the room, winding his way through our boots. He found his way to Top, lay down using Top's boot as a headrest, and let out a sigh as if to say, "I'm here."

Afterward, Fred showed up right as I sat down on my sleeping mat. I untied my boots and left them beside me, stacking my pants on top so I could jump in at a moment's notice. Next to them were my body armor, my helmet, a bandolier, magazines, a rifle, and my camera. I took off my watch, laying it next to my pillow, and when I swung my legs around to lie back, Fred leapt in, too, and made himself at home. He took a couple of turns, pawed at the sleeping bag a little, then eventually settled in between my legs, resting his head on my thigh. As a kid, sometimes our family cat, Patches, would sleep in the same spot, curled between my knees. Having Fred there felt familiar, like a little piece of my old life.

In Sangin, that's what Fred offered all of us. Each time he curled up in one of our sleeping bags—there were a few times he cuddled up with Top or Dave, an EOD guy—or trotted across the compound or let us scratch him behind the ears, we got an escape from the combat zone we were in. In those moments, it was just you and Fred.

The next day, I was on a rooftop post looking through my binoculars into the green fields in the distance.

One of the guys said, "Hey, look."

I pulled my binoculars away and looked down to where he was pointing. A man and woman were walking right by our compound, maybe thirty feet away. He was walking in front of her, and she was following behind, leading their donkey, which carried bags of rice, rugs, and buckets on its back.

We were happy to see them. We hadn't seen villagers come so close to the compound, and after days of firefights, it seemed like a good sign that people were out in the middle of the day. Maybe we'd driven away enough Taliban for them to regain some freedom of movement.

Then we heard a loud, eruptive thud. You could feel it in your gut, like a clap of thunder. I flinched, ducking my head, and looked out to where the couple had been. I saw the man standing in his long white shirt and pants, motionless. Behind him, where the woman and donkey had been, a black cloud of smoke rose from the ground. The caustic smell of ammonia hung in the air. The hair on my arms stood up. We knew instinctively: she'd stepped on an IED.

I quickly climbed down from the roof. Below, Ali was already talking with some of the Afghan commandos and a few marines. Ali was convinced we should go speak with the man. In spite of the impossible difficulty of the moment, we needed to make sure he knew it wasn't coalition forces that had killed his wife. We could also help him. In the Islamic religion, a dead body should only be handled by another Muslim. Because Ali and the Afghan commandos were Muslim, they could offer to help gather remains. One of the Afghan commandos went to get a bedsheet. I put on my kit, and we walked out.

After the explosion, the man had stood for a while, looking at the blast site, frozen. Now he was moving about, beginning to collect what remained of his wife. The commandos approached him with the sheet and offered to help. Ali joined them, telling him how sorry we were. The man, understandably, began to seem delirious. He spoke rapidly, and I lost track of what the conversation was about or what was being said. For a long time, the men spoke in Pashto. I waited nearby, tense and hot.

When it felt like the right moment, I stepped in next to Ali. Ali told me a little bit in English, but nothing was making sense. I offered my condolences and gently made sure to reiterate that the man's wife had been killed by a Taliban IED. He understood. The villagers in Sangin knew what the Taliban were doing and what they were capable of.

I sucked in a lungful of air and, feeling sick, made a final request. It was my job to record and report Taliban-inflicted casualties. I asked if I could photograph the body. The man agreed. When he opened the bedsheet, a few flies buzzed out. The woman's head was turned away, so I couldn't see her face. One arm was gone from the elbow down; the other was still there, but with no fingers. Her legs, if they were still there, were obscured by her dress.

My chest was so tight it was hard to breathe. I felt like I might vomit. I took a couple of photos, using all my willpower to remain composed.

Back in the compound, we gathered to talk. In the field, our brains are wired for work and for survival. Something troubling became clear: there were IEDs much closer to our compound than we'd realized. We'd practically walked over that same area on our way out for night patrols. The reality was that we were likely surrounded by many more of them.

As we were talking, I spotted Fred. He came trotting across the compound with his head held high. He had something in his mouth. If you've ever seen a dog with a new toy—totally gleeful and proud, practically squirming with joy—that's how Fred looked. He plopped down and started gnawing, happy as ever. Then I realized what it was: a charred piece of donkey leg, from the hoof to the knee, almost as big as he was.

"Ugh, Fred!" I ran over and pulled the thing from his mouth, throwing it over the wall. "No!" I shouted, sternly, looking at his confused puppy face.

The next day, though, I found the stinking, rotting leg at the end of my sleeping bag. I picked it up and threw it over the wall again, hoping that was the end of it. But Fred somehow found it, once again, and brought it back in. Over the next few days, he continued to leave it around the compound, sometimes on different guys' sleeping mats, and we continued throwing it over the wall, partly disgusted, partly amused. It was hard to be too mad. Fred didn't know anything about the Taliban or tragedy or war. It was that innocence—especially in the dark moments—that buoyed us.

CHAPTER 5

The Delta Blues

By the time Josh and I finally arrived in Chattanooga, it was nearly dusk. The mountains gave way to sprawling city blocks, and it wasn't long before we found ourselves at a bar on a big, open lot that looked like it had once been a service station. Tables and lounge areas were scattered around, along with yard games like cornhole and oversize Jenga. We sat with my buddy Mike and a group of his friends on a cluster of outdoor sofas. Fred jumped right up onto a couch and made himself at home.

Mike—or Mikey, as I used to call him—and I had been friends since childhood. We met in elementary school, and by high school, we were skipping class together. Mikey would jump into my beat-up '89 Mazda and we'd drive back to my house, climb out my bedroom window, and sit on the garage roof while Mike burned through a pack of cigarettes in an hour. I guess it was our form of seventeen-year-old suburban-kid rebellion. I hadn't seen Mike in years, but we had one of those friendships where you could pick up right where you left off.

We ate dinner at a place near Mike's house and caught up over fried chicken and forty-ounce beers. Afterward, we headed to the outdoor bar, passing by old southern homes with wide porches and green lawns. Streetlamps lined the sidewalks, and the summer night was warm. Mike and Josh walked up ahead, talking and getting to know each other while Fred and I followed. I smiled seeing one of my childhood friends walking side by side with one of my newest buddies.

At the bar, we got into a game of Jenga while we all talked and drank. I was carefully working to slide one of the big blocks of wood from its place in the Jenga tower when Clint, one of Mike's friends, asked me the question.

"So, what kind of dog is Fred?" Clint sat down next to the dog, petting him behind the ears.

I smiled as I slid the block free and placed it on top of the now wobbling tower. By this time, I'd been home from Afghanistan for a few years, and I'd gotten used to people stopping me on the street or in the dog park to ask about my dog. Fred didn't look like other dogs, and he was charismatic. People were drawn to him. Sometimes he'd make eye contact with someone on the sidewalk, and next thing I knew, the person would say, "Oh my gosh, where did you get this dog?" I told the truth.

"Well, I actually found him in Afghanistan a few years ago. He was way too cool to leave behind," I said.

Clint looked up at me. Between the memorial bracelets we wore, Josh's prosthetic, and my cutoff camo shorts, we weren't fooling anyone—it was clear Josh and I were vets. Still, I don't think Clint expected me to bring up Afghanistan like that. As the silence stretched on, Mike stepped in.

"Fred has a great story," he said. "He followed you around on patrols, right, man?"

I started telling the guys a little bit about where I found Fred, describing Sangin and our mission there. I told them how amazed we'd been at Fred's friendly behavior in the compound. It wasn't like he'd come upon our base looking for handouts. We had landed right in Fred's territory, and even though he probably hadn't had any positive human interaction before, he welcomed us.

As I talked, Fred napped on the sofa next to me.

When I finished the story, I reached for my beer and drank the rest of it down. I liked having the opportunity to talk about Afghanistan in a way people—especially civilians—wouldn't necessarily expect. Battling assumptions is something every vet has to deal with, and it can be really frustrating, particularly when you get the sense someone wants to know if you're "okay." I don't mind answering questions when they come from an earnest place, but it's never a simple task. Sometimes someone at a bar asks, "What's it like over there?" as if they're just asking about the weather. Then you have to come up with a way to fit the answer—this big, complicated, messy thing—neatly and casually into a few sentences. You keep it light because you don't have any other choice. Occasionally, though, you get a chance to elaborate. That's what Fred's story allowed me to do: to say more, to get into detail. Fred, oblivious to the attention he was receiving, lay there napping peacefully.

While I'd been talking, a couple of clean-cut guys had wandered over from the bar and stood within earshot. They were big guys, tall, with muscular builds. There was something about their posture—plus their clean shaves, cropped haircuts, and polo shirts—that was a dead giveaway. They were marines.

After I finished my story, the two clean-cut guys walked up and introduced themselves. As I guessed, they said they were infantry marines with tours in Iraq and Afghanistan. Their names were Eric and Paul, and they had both recently separated from the marines and moved back to Tennessee for school.

Paul, who had a big smile and cowboy boots that made him stand substantially taller than me, offered to buy Josh and me a beer. I held up my empty and said, "You read my mind."

With that, the four of us made our way to the bar. The guys were regulars, so we had our fresh beers within seconds, even though the bar was crowded.

"Cheers," we said, lifting our drinks. We didn't need to say who we were toasting: now that we were home, any time we raised a glass with fellow marines, it was understood we were drinking to the friends who hadn't made it back.

"Did you lose your leg in combat, sir?" Eric said, turning to Josh.

"Yup," Josh said, taking a gulp of his drink. "I put it down in the middle of a firefight and forgot where I left it." Eric and Paul both grinned. Josh's sense of humor about his injury always put people at ease. "And don't call me sir," he added. "I was an enlisted guy just like you."

We talked about where we'd been and what our roles were over there, about being home and going to college as vets. But soon enough, the conversation turned to Fred.

"I can't believe you got Fred outta there, man. It's good to hear someone was able to pull it off," Paul said. "When we were over there, we had Maisy."

"She was the best," Eric added. The two marines explained

how their unit had come across Maisy on one of their deployments in Afghanistan. Just like Fred, she'd become a companion to the marines, even sleeping with them at night when it got cold, curled up on their mats. They laughed when they saw Fred's fluffy butt and expressive tail, just like Maisy's. She had been bigger than Fred, though, with long legs, a furry, speckled coat, and a build that sounded like an Australian shepherd's.

Eric and Paul had worked in route security, which meant they had the harrowing task of driving down village streets all day, never knowing if the road beneath them would erupt. They patrolled the well-established routes that were used to move supplies from base to base, but the fact that the roads were routinely traveled by coalition forces made them susceptible to attacks. It meant the Taliban knew, more or less, when you were coming and where you were going. It's the kind of job that can go from really boring to really bad in an instant. And if a truck in the convoy got hit, you had to get out of your vehicle to go pull guys out, leaving everyone exposed and vulnerable.

I could see how much having a dog on a mission like that would help defuse anxiety. After long days on the road, Maisy was there to greet them when they returned from patrols, and sometimes she'd even follow their M-ATVs when they convoyed from base to base.

"She always found us, no matter how far we moved or how hot it got," Paul said. He lifted his beer to his mouth, took a swig, and looked off.

By the way they were talking, I knew what was coming.

Paul said the unit had made their way to a permanent base and began conducting patrols out of it. When Maisy followed them there, they created a little bed for her out of some old pillows and blankets. She even had a collar they made out of woven paracord. The unit had gotten so attached to her that they'd begun the formal process of requesting permission to have her sponsored by a U.S. nonprofit that could help get her home.

Then one day, while out on patrol, the guys were ambushed. The whole platoon came under fierce machine gun fire, and one of their teammates was shot and killed. During the ambush, they suspected he'd been targeted by a sniper. It was a grueling, devastating day.

They got back to their base, completely drained, expecting to be greeted by the dog's happy prances and tail wags, the kind of positivity only a dog can bring to a place like that. But her bed was empty and Maisy wasn't around. There'd been a few other stray dogs on the base, too, and they weren't there, either. The place was quiet. Something was off.

The guys slowly put it together: while they were out patrolling, the command had ordered the dogs to be euthanized.

Eric and Paul weren't shy about their emotions. Their voices were tight and they each wiped the corners of their eyes with the backs of their hands. I looked over at Fred, who was still stretched out on the couch, lifting his head every so often to greet a stranger and receive a pet. It wasn't the first time I'd heard a story like this one. In a combat zone, some commands considered dogs a threat to good order and discipline. There were a lot of fears about diseases, and in a case like Maisy's, the big worry was that she could become a dangerous distraction—one that could compromise the focus and integrity of a unit. What if the unit was put in a situation where one of the guys risked his life—or the life of a fellow marine—to protect the dog? The fact that Maisy was perceived more as a liability than as an asset was a bitter reality of war. In Sangin, my biggest fear was that the same would happen to Fred.

"I'm so sorry, man," I said. I knew they would understand that I wasn't just talking about the dog, but about the teammate they lost—about all our lost friends.

Josh stepped over to the bar and ordered each of us a shot of Jameson. The four of us raised the small glasses of amber liquid into the air.

"To Maisy," I said.

"To Fred," the guys replied. We knocked back the whiskey. The familiar burn in my throat matched the sting in my eyes. I think I said something to Paul and Eric about how the dog had still served a purpose, how the joy Maisy brought to their unit would stay with them forever. I believed that wholeheartedly, and I meant it. But, looking at Fred, I felt a pit in my stomach. If he'd met the same fate, I hated to think of what it would have done to me.

Back in Afghanistan, Fred had been my companion and comfort, but now that I was home, he was starting to play another role, too. In everyday life, out at some bar, it could feel impossible to swap stories about the buddies we'd lost. How do you even start a conversation like that? Fred gave us a place to begin, a way to talk about some of the things we didn't want to say but probably needed to. He gave us a way to talk about war.

Early Monday morning, when the grass was still wet with dew and the sun was just starting to come up over the mountains,

Josh and I loaded up the Land Cruiser and got ready to return to the road. The rest of the weekend had gone by fast. Mike showed us around the city and took us hiking on a few of his favorite trails. As we said good-bye, I promised him we'd try to come through Chattanooga again on the way back.

Back in the truck, Josh and I set our sights southwest. Our next city destination was Austin, Texas, but we wanted to make a few stops along the way. In Mississippi, we hoped to catch some authentic blues music and do some camping.

The drive was steady and hot. We avoided highways as much as possible. The Land Cruiser never wanted to go much over fifty-five, but we weren't in a hurry. We stuck to little two-lane byways and rural routes, crossing through small, sleepy towns where people sat on their porches watching us go by. Old folks and younger ones, in baseball caps or cowboy hats, wearing dirty sneakers or boots with worn soles, or no shoes at all. They sat and squinted and smoked. We passed by dilapidated mills, boarded-up factories, and ghost-quiet Main Streets. Whenever the truck slowed, Fred popped up in the backseat to see what the change in pace was about. He'd yawn and stretch, stick his nose out the window, then poke his head between us for a wind-shield view. Once satisfied, he'd curl up again and wait for the next stop.

Clarksdale, Mississippi, is nestled in the heart of the Missis-sippi Delta, just ten miles from the big river to the west and an afternoon's drive from Memphis in the north and Jackson in the south. The town was in our path, and we knew only one thing about it: Morgan Freeman ran a juke joint downtown. It's where we decided we'd go to hear the blues with the locals.

We rolled into town just before dinner and pulled over at

the first cheap motel we spotted. The modest two-story building sat on a mostly empty, sun-bleached parking lot where tufts of grass pushed through cracks in the concrete. A tall sign out front flashed VACANCY in illuminated red script. We parked in front of the office and got out. I left the windows down, and when Fred stuck his head out, I looked at him and said, "Stay here, buddy."

Inside the office, a flat-screen TV on low volume flickered to our right; to the left was a tall front counter. From a small office area behind the desk, I heard the unmistakable squeal of metal springs on a cot, then a small man came through the doorway, wiping the sleep from his eyes. He could barely see over the tall counter between us, but he smiled and got to work checking us in, making sure to tell us about the free breakfast in the lobby.

Handing me the key, he chirped once more, "Breakfast in the morning! Six to nine!"

"Thank you," I said, smiling back at the clerk before pushing through the door again. We rejoined Fred and moved the truck down to the parking spot in front of our first-level door.

Inside, the room was clean, with two double beds and an old bubble TV. After feeding Fred and washing up, Josh and I headed back out again, eager to get to the juke joint.

The bar sat on a narrow road in an industrial part of town. The building might have been able to pass for an abandoned warehouse were it not for the steady stream of tourists making their way through the front door. The sound of muffled live music seeped out from inside. On a wide porch out front, a man checked our IDs, and in we went, the music hitting us like a wave as we entered.

We got a seat at the bar and ordered two Budweisers, which came frothy and cold in glasses. I put the beer to my lips and looked around, taking in the place. The walls were covered with license plates, strings of colored lights, guitars, flags, and an assortment of signs. Beneath all that were handwritten signatures scrawled onto walls by visitors with black Sharpie pens. Everything was made to look a certain way—old, authentic, rugged—but I could see how each item had been arranged intentionally. It was all more themed than authentic, kind of like a Hard Rock Cafe. Around us sat older retired couples, tapping their feet and swaying awkwardly. I was starting to feel like we'd stumbled upon an AARP retreat in a chain restaurant.

The band onstage, however, was the real deal. Under colorful lights that hung overhead, the musicians hummed together like a well-oiled machine. The lead singer and guitarist, with his deep, soulful voice, looked like he'd been at it for a long time. Josh and I didn't know much about blues, but we knew what we were hearing was good. As we worked through our second beer, I looked at Josh, like, "You good?" and he nodded. We were tired, and a clean motel room with basic cable sounded pretty nice.

As we walked down the alley toward the Land Cruiser, the muffled music from behind us was replaced by the sound of another band coming from somewhere up ahead. It was late, but the one thing we'd wanted to do in Clarksdale was to hang out at a juke joint, and neither of us had been satisfied with the canned atmosphere at the last place. So we followed the sound to its source, just to see where it led. Making our way down the alley, we found the squat brick building that was home to a howling guitar. No one was around, but an old meat smoker sat out front, under a red light that hung over the metal door. When I pulled the door open, music and light flooded out, casting shadows onto the pavement.

The bar was a single, small room where everything glowed red. Metal chairs with red vinyl cushions and a few shabby tables were scattered around, and the walls were covered with posters and signs that looked like they'd been there a long time. The sagging ceiling was low enough to reach up and touch. There was no stage—just a rug on the ground where an old guy in a blue suit and tie leaned back in a wobbly chair, plucking away at the guitar. He must've been in his eighties, but his fingers moved like lightning over the strings as if the instrument were a part of him. Behind him, a drummer played along.

There couldn't have been more than a dozen people inside, and everyone turned as we stepped through the door. Once inside, though, we were committed. We walked over to the bar, where a big black guy wearing sunglasses stood behind the counter.

"Hey, man. Can we get a couple beers?" I asked.

From behind the bar, he opened a plastic Igloo cooler, pulled out two forties of Bud, and placed them in front of us. It was a taller order than expected, but it didn't seem like the kind of place to dispute what you'd been given. I paid the three bucks for each, smiling and thanking the man. "This is a great spot," I added. "Glad we found it."

Knowingly, the bartender grinned. "Y'all come from that other bar?"

"We did," I said. "Didn't really feel like sticking around."

"This is my place. The name's Red," he said.

Josh and I extended our hands and introduced ourselves. Then Red got a look at Josh's prosthetic. His face changed, and with genuine awe, he said, "You're wearing shorts?"

Josh smiled. "Yeah, man!" he said. "It's hot as hell down here."

Red told us he had a cousin who'd also lost his leg. But he'd been too embarrassed to wear anything but long pants ever since, no matter how hot it got.

"If I got him down here, would you talk to him?" Red said, looking at Josh.

"Of course," Josh said. Within a few minutes, Red's cousin showed up. He was much taller and looked younger than Red, with dreadlocks that fell below his shoulders. He seemed a little uncomfortable on his prosthetic and used a wooden cane. We got the impression that maybe he was still getting the hang of life with one leg. Coming through the door, he spotted us right away and introduced himself as Riley.

Red pointed to Josh and said, "See? Shorts!"

Riley shook Josh's hand. His smile and eye contact were so sincere—almost nervous. I wondered if, living in this small town, he'd met many other people with prosthetics before.

"How'd you lose yours?" Riley asked.

"My vehicle hit a roadside bomb in Afghanistan a few years ago. Haven't seen it since," Josh replied.

Riley paused for a moment, looking slightly uncomfortable. But Josh quickly added, "Let's see what you've got going on. Red says you're a fellow member of the peg-leg club."

Riley smiled and bent forward, gently rolling up the leg of his jeans. Unlike Josh, you could see that he had his knee, but below it was a carbon fiber tube attached to a shock absorber ankle and a foot that went into the black sneakers he wore. Airbrushed right onto the shin of the prosthetic was the unmistakable blue and silver star of a Dallas Cowboys logo.

"Aha! I see why you wear pants all the time with that thing painted on your leg," Josh teased. Red and Riley both laughed.

Josh asked Riley about his experience with his leg, then offered his advice on prosthetic maintenance and care. Josh sat right on the floor and removed his leg completely to show Riley the kind of sock he used to help stop chafing and irritation, as well as telling him about the kind of cream he found worked best. Even though Josh had had his prosthetic for over five years and had plenty of tips, he knew from experience how vulnerable a single leg could make you feel, especially with follow-up surgeries that made it difficult to gain momentum. "Healing can mean two steps forward, one back," he said.

As Josh and Riley exchanged the quick back-and-forth banter of two men who truly understood each other's situation, I could tell they had a real connection.

"Seeing you walk around . . . it's unbelievable," Riley said. "I never would have thought I could wear shorts."

"It's a hundred degrees here!" Josh said. "There's nothing to be ashamed of."

Josh sat on a chair next to Riley and demonstrated how his prosthetic could swivel 360 degrees at the knee so that, sitting down, he could spin the foot into the air and rest his beer on the sole of his shoe.

By now the band had wrapped up for the night and most of the patrons had shuffled out. The four of us stayed and talked well past closing.

When we finally got ready to go, we shook the guys' hands, and Red said with sincerity, "Y'all are welcome back any time."

Like Fred, Josh's prosthetic was a way to talk about war. Unlike me, though, war was visible on Josh's body. Anywhere he went, he'd get questions about what happened to his leg. Even if his time in Afghanistan wasn't overtly discussed every time, there was an opening to talk about it, if Josh wanted to. That's what Fred did for me, too. If I didn't have him, no one would guess that I was a combat veteran, and there wouldn't be that chance to connect with people in quite the same way. I loved talking about Fred and how we found one another— the fact that it happened in a place that a lot of people are unfamiliar and uncomfortable with made it more fun to share.

Coming home, one of the biggest challenges vets face is this overwhelming sense of isolation—feeling like you're alone, like no one gets it. For those of us who separated from active duty, it was easy to suddenly find ourselves without direction. Even if you found a job or went to school, what could compare to the camaraderie and sense of purpose that came with serving during a time of war? Where do you go from there? Trying to figure that out was a big reason Josh and I were on the road. But the more people Josh and I talked to, the less isolated we felt. Even if the people across from us didn't know much about Afghanistan—even if we were the first vets they'd met—for a short time, we shared something, and it felt good. One of the symptoms of isolation is a feeling that people just don't care, that they aren't interested in your experiences or your pain, but we were starting to see that that just wasn't true.

CHAPTER 6

The Green Zone

We continued to patrol at night, falling into a routine. Our three platoons rotated duties. One platoon would keep post on the rooftops; another would rest, prepared to be a quick reaction force (QRF) if anything happened; and one would go out into the Green Zone. Meanwhile, Ali and I patrolled every night; I wanted to build relationships with as many villagers as possible. It was strategic for us to have positive face-to-face interactions with these families so that if and when they acquired information about the Taliban, they'd be more likely to tell us. We didn't want the villagers to think of us as a mysterious, robotic force sitting behind weapons up on a hill. On patrols, we had a chance to introduce ourselves as real people, here to help.

Once, Ali and I climbed into a compound, using a ladder, and startled an older man as he walked across the courtyard. "It's okay, Grandfather," Ali said in Pashto. "We're here to talk." We came over the walls, with a few other RECON guys on the roof, and the old man brought his family to the courtyard, where we all sat in a circle. There were nine or ten people gathered. I took the night vision from my helmet and handed it to one of the kids. She was amazed by how it worked. She lifted it to her face, then pulled it away, then looked through it again, smiling in disbelief. One of her brothers took it and started doing the same. A teenage boy passed around chai tea. From my pack, I took out photos of my family, explaining that they were my parents and sister. I had this one picture of my sister, Sarah, holding her dog, Herbie, a little terrier mix with short, shiny brown hair, a smooshed snout, and a peppy personality. For whatever reason, the Afghan villagers always found the picture of Herbie hilarious. This group was no exception. The kids giggled at the little dog, cracking up till they lost their breath.

I told them we were here because we knew the Taliban were making their lives difficult, and we wanted to help—we wanted them to be able to open schools and shops again, to live normal lives. We knew that in small villages like this, the Taliban spread insidious rumors about us. Sometimes, if villagers had any awareness of the September 11 attacks, their understanding was that they were in retaliation for our presence in the country, not the other way around. I'd first heard about this piece of Taliban propaganda in intel reports. It shocked me. I realized the extent to which the Taliban were manipulating people—not just through horrific violence but through heinous misinformation, too.

When we had a chance to talk with people like this family, though, I was always amazed by their kindness and understanding. They were receptive; they listened and asked questions. And they were grateful. It gave me hope that our mission was meaningful and would have a real impact on people. The conversations helped me, too. I enjoyed them. Even with the language barrier, I found I could connect with people. Sometimes, just talking with villagers, I no longer felt like we were in a battle zone. Even though their houses looked different from my own, I felt welcomed, and the feeling of being in someone's home was familiar and comforting.

As the patrols went on, the days started to run together. I wrote reports each morning after returning from patrols and recorded the villages we visited, most of which weren't on any map. I'd try to nap, but between the heat and Taliban attacks, I was often interrupted. The day would slip by, and when the sun would set, I'd line up my gear along the wall and get ready for the next patrol. By the time I returned to the compound each night, in the late hours just before morning broke, Top would gently tease me as I walked through the door. "Here comes the mayor!" he'd say, because I was always patrolling.

After his first expedition out, Fred continued to follow me on night patrols. He'd silently trot alongside our patrol line, about thirty feet to our left or right, stopping when we stopped, crossing canals when we crossed canals, and struggling up muddy banks right alongside us. He was so quiet and agile that no one questioned his company. He didn't distract us or interfere with our work. Instead, he was a comfort, our little patrol dog looking out for us.

One night, however, that changed. On our way to a village in the Green Zone, the patrol cut through a cornfield. The corn in Sangin was American corn, and the stalks were twice our height and as close together as the hair on our heads. It was perfect cover for moving around undetected. It was also perfect for getting lost in. As we walked through, each member of the patrol had to keep an eye on the guy in front of him; otherwise, you could easily get disoriented or even lost among the stalks. Because the corn was so dense and difficult to navigate, Fred didn't follow us in. Instead, he found a path around the field so he could meet us on the other side. It made me nervous. One wrong step and Fred could go up in pieces.

As we emerged through the corn, we confronted a wide expanse of barren fields. The fields must have stretched out for a hundred acres, arranged in a grid, each section bordered by narrow raised pathways. The open space was less than ideal. There was nothing to cover us, and the moon shone in the sky, making the night brighter than usual. Out in the open, we were pretty much sitting ducks. A single Taliban fighter would have no problem taking out multiple members of our patrol. We got on the move, quickly.

Fred, meanwhile, safely materialized off our flank, trotting along on his own path. But as I watched him, I heard a strange, unfamiliar sound shatter the quiet of the night. It took a second for me to register what it was: Fred barking. Stunned, I watched as his trot turned into a bolt and he came barreling across the field. He zipped through our patrol line and kept going, howling at something up ahead.

Instinctively, we all took a knee, raised our guns, and scanned the horizon. Not only were we totally exposed, but now we had a dog calling attention to our position. One of the marines raised his rifle and aimed it at Fred. Through my night vision, I could see the infrared light from the end of his gun illuminate the dog in the dark.

Frantically, I reached into the dirt around me, searching for a stone or clump of soil to throw at Fred to get him to snap out of it and shut up. My fingers found only dust. Fred kept barking.

Then, with the infrared light shining on Fred, we could see something beyond him that must've been the reason for his barks. In the next field over, I made out a dark wool blanket stretched out across the ground.

I looked over at Ali, who saw it, too. "Let's go," I said, and we moved toward it as the marines fanned out, some with their rifles aimed toward the blanket, others scanning the horizon. Ali and I jogged past Fred, who stood back, growling.

One of the guys grabbed Fred by the scruff to make sure he stayed put. Reaching for a dried cornstalk lying on the ground, he picked it up and used it as a tug-of-war toy to distract the dog.

As Ali and I got closer, it was clear there were people underneath the blanket. Ali shouted for them to come out, and two young men stood up. We separated them for questioning. They claimed to be farmers, showing us the small hand shovels they were carrying. But they couldn't answer any of our simple questions about the fields, like what they were planting or how long they'd worked in the village. It was obvious they were IED emplacers sent to plant bombs at night. We took their pictures, then released them. We weren't equipped to take prisoners, and they didn't have anything incriminating on them for me to justify the risk and effort to detain them.

The encounter made me worry that the Taliban knew about our night patrols and were keeping track of our movements. If they knew we were avoiding paths and cutting through fields, they'd lay their booby traps accordingly. One thing was definitely clear: Fred's time patrolling with us was over. I couldn't have him putting us—and him—in that position again if we were all going to survive this mission.

The next night, when we lined up at the door to head out, Fred scampered between us excitedly as he always did, ready for his nightly outing. As we ducked through our tiny doorway, Top counted us one by one, tapping us on the back as he always did. When I came through the door with Fred on my heels, Top reached down and grabbed him by his scruff. "Not anymore, buddy," he said. "You're on radio duty with me now."

For the rest of our time in Sangin, Fred waited in the compound each night with Top, assuming his new position as greeter in chief.

In the Green Zone, canals crisscrossed through the fields endlessly, like a maze. Usually the canals were obstacles—we'd have to find a way to cross them, either with two long wooden posts side by side, shimmying across like the farmers did, or by wading through. Sometimes, though, we'd encounter empty canals that could be used as pathways. At about five feet deep, they provided great cover, and they were unlikely to contain IEDs since they were frequently flooded with water.

One night, we were cutting through a dry canal when we spotted people moving above us in the adjacent field. We were shocked. We rarely saw anyone out in the dead of night, and if we did, more often than not, we had reason to shoot them. Through our night vision, we watched a military-age man walking swiftly, followed by five or six young boys. The man carried a pillowcase sack over his shoulder, and the whole crew had the same sort of posture—bent forward as if sneaking around, moving quickly. Taliban IED emplacers, we thought.

The Taliban routinely used kids to place IEDs. On my previous mission, in Trek Nawa, I once watched from our rooftop post as a Taliban fighter drove into a neighboring compound on a motorcycle, a young boy sitting in front of him and another sitting behind. Hanging over the side was a bag with a soccer ball inside. Once they drove into the compound, they were obscured from sight. Next thing I knew, five kids came bounding out, excitedly kicking the soccer ball between them. As they played, I watched one of the boys from the motorcycle start to dig a hole using a small garden trowel. Inside, he dropped a jug—a telltale canister of homemade explosives—and covered it up. The other boy from the motorcycle carried the pressure plate. He dug a shallow hole right next to the jug and carefully connected it with wires. The whole thing only took a couple of minutes; it was clear they were well trained. With the job done, the guy on the motorcycle emerged from the compound again. The boys quickly got on, and they drove away. Not only did the Taliban use the kids to do their work and serve as their body armor, but the whole method made it impossible for us to interfere. If we shot that Taliban fighter, it would have been in front of a group of young kids who probably viewed him as a good guy—someone who'd given them a soccer ball.

Typically, though, the Taliban weren't so obvious. Most IEDs were planted at night. Sometimes a network of IEDs lay dormant and disconnected during the day, for the safety of the farmers, and were then activated at night. When they were connected like that, we called them daisy-chained. Step on one and the whole network would go off.

From the canal, we watched the group come closer. I turned to Ali and the nearest marine to me, and said, "Come on." We ducked into a canal running perpendicular to ours and ran down it while the rest of the guys fanned out. I was certain the guy we had spotted had bribed the boys with candy, or threatened them, and now was walking them around all night, sending them into fields to dig holes and plant bombs. We were going to put an end to that right now.

The canal was narrow, only about three feet wide, and we moved quickly, trying not to let our gear noisily scrape the sides. The group was ahead of us now, and the canal came right up alongside their path overhead. My heart raced. As we silently ran up to their position, us down in the canal, them on the pathway above, I hoisted myself up over the edge and reached for the man with my right hand, grasping his shirt near the collar and pulling him down into the canal while the RECON marine corralled the boys.

"WHO THE FUCK ARE YOU?" I shouted.

I pinned him down in the dirt with my knee, bearing down on his chest. I leaned toward his face so he could see my eyes.

"Who are you?" I growled. "Are you Taliban?" I spat the words, not waiting for an answer.

The man couldn't have been very old—maybe in his twenties

or thirties. He had a black beard and a shaved head. Most of the men we met in Afghanistan grew their hair out through the seasons, then buzzed it off once each year. I could tell he had just shaved his because his scalp was still raw and pink. He wore plastic sandals, a dusty white robe, loose pants, and a tan vest.

Stunned, he was stumbling over his words, eventually gathering more momentum as he repeated a phrase again and again that I didn't understand. Before Ali could translate, the RECON guy reached down and grabbed me by the shoulder.

"Look at this," he said.

He was pointing to the sack the guy had been carrying, opening it so I could see inside. Beside him, the kids were stunned silent. They were young, maybe between six and nine years old, and they sat huddled together. The whites of their wide, fearful eyes were bright in the moonlight.

I peered inside the sack, expecting to find homemade explosives, wires, pliers. Instead, it was full of books. Confused, I pulled them out. There were math books, religion books, notebooks, pencils. School supplies.

I turned back to the man. We looked at each other for a moment, then I took my knee off his chest and pulled him up so he could sit. Ali and I brushed the dirt from his back.

"I'm a teacher," he was saying in Pashto, tears in his eyes. "A schoolteacher."

I'd never heard the word *teacher* in Pashto before.

"I'm so sorry," I said, stunned. "We thought you were Taliban."

Ali and one of the guys helped the kids down into the canal for cover, and we sat and talked.

"You're a teacher?" I asked, and Ali began to interpret his words. The man told us his name was Asif. He and his older brother had created a makeshift schoolhouse in a compound in the nearby village. It was just a small room tucked away in a house where kids sat on a rug on the floor. At night, Asif and his brother would make their way through the surrounding villages and gather children, bringing them back to the schoolhouse to teach them under the dim light of an oil lamp. They had to hide because the Taliban prohibited any form of education. No books. No music. No writing. No school.

"If the Taliban find out, they will kill me," Asif said. "Like they killed my brother."

In Pashto, the word for Taliban is simply *Talib,* so I could always make it out, even before Ali translated.

About a month earlier, Asif said, the Taliban had somehow found out what he and his brother were up to. They captured both brothers, then forced them onto their knees side by side. They shot his brother in the head and left Asif to bear the message.

I looked over at the kids, who were still sitting quietly, watching us. They hadn't said a word this entire time. I doubt they'd ever interacted with someone from the military before. They looked so terrified and small.

I tried to find out about Asif's brother's killers, but Asif didn't know much. He remembered four or five men but didn't know who they were. After that night, he'd never seen them again.

Between the damp walls of the canal, everything smelled like earth. The sky above was dark, still.

Trying to focus, I told Asif it was dangerous at night, that it wasn't safe to move around in the fields with the kids. "We could have shot you," I said.

He looked at me. His eyes had dried, and his voice was calm and measured. "I'm not going to stop teaching," he said. "Whether you kill me or the Taliban do."

My eyes met his, and I understood there was nothing I could say to try to convince him.

"Please, just stay in one place, at least for tonight," I pleaded. He pointed to a village nearby, saying they weren't going much farther.

We helped Asif and the boys out of the canal and returned their things. As they continued through the night, the books slung over Asif's shoulders, the patrol watched them till they reached their destination.

Back at the compound that night, as I lay on my mat with Fred curled up between my legs, I couldn't stop thinking about the schoolteacher and his brother, about the children huddled in the ditch of the canal, their wide eyes. Our mission in Sangin was to beat back the Taliban, clear IEDs, make the area safe, and hopefully, eventually, supply electricity. I thought of all the money and resources that were being poured into the country. All the weapons. But was that really what those kids needed from us? Sometimes I wasn't sure.

Each day, from sunup to sundown, Taliban bullets and bombs crashed in and around our compound. But I felt the threat of the Taliban most deeply when I met people like Asif. Here was someone who had every right to retreat into despair, anger, and fear, yet instead, in the midst of the horror, he had staked his claim on the world, pledging to make it better.

On one particularly hot day, Fred and I took refuge from the sun under a makeshift tarp awning. Sangin's afternoon heat could be brutal, and this was one of the worst waves yet. The day was quiet and oppressive, with no activity from the Taliban. It was as if everyone in the desert were suffocating.

Under the tarp, I wiped the sweat from my forehead and finished up a report while Fred snoozed nearby. As I typed in my final notes, I caught sight of an Afghan commando pacing around the compound. The commandos from the Afghan National Army had been embedded with us to help communicate with the villagers and contribute to our mission. Jason, a royal marine, was training them.

Sometimes, the commandos were an invaluable resource—they had cultural insight and interpretation capabilities that we lacked, and they could be great liaisons between us and the villagers. In Trek Nawa, we worked with a group of ANA guys who were incredible. They patrolled with us frequently and one of them, a teenager named Ali, volunteered to be an interpreter when our Ali needed a break. He was a talented, hardworking kid who had learned English from watching bootleg American movies.

In Sangin, though, the ANA group had a different mentality. From the start, they had disagreed with our approach of patrolling at night—it seemed too risky to them—and so they didn't join us. But since our night patrols made up most of our activity, that left the commandos with very little to do. They spent most of their days inside the walls of the compound, and without electricity, running water, good food, or jobs to perform, a few of them started to seem sick of it all.

The member of the ANA team that I had my eye on was notoriously vocal about his frustrations—the monotony, the heat, the lack of work. At one point, after seeing one of us give Fred a bite to eat, he exclaimed, "How can you marines expect respect when you treat this disgusting dog like he is person?" Usually, we just ignored him. He had a way of getting ornery in the heat, and we also understood that taking care of Fred probably did seem a little strange to him and the other Afghan commandos. We weren't in a part of Afghanistan where it was customary to have pets. When it came to Fred, most of the ANA guys either didn't pay him much attention or just shook their heads and laughed when they saw us taking care of him. One of the commandos, a nice guy who spoke English, once walked by while Fred was sleeping on my mat. "He's in your bed? Aren't you mad?" he asked me, smiling curiously. Treating the dusty critter like a companion who had full rein of our sleeping quarters probably seemed crazy to them.

As usual, the commando I was watching pace the compound looked irritated. In his dark green cammies and heavy boots, he huffed around kicking up dirt. Fred, who was having a tough time staying cool, got up and sauntered toward his dirt patch under the bushes. As I watched their paths start to converge, I held my breath. Before I could really think about what was happening, the commando shifted his weight onto his left leg, lifted his right, and sent it swinging into Fred's rib cage. The force of the kick lifted Fred off his paws. He let out a loud whimper, spun around, and looked up at the commando in confusion.

Before I could react, one of the EOD guys on the mission,

Dave, jumped up and got in the commando's face. Dave was a tough-looking guy from Michigan with a MADE IN DETROIT tattoo across his wrist. He was an attachment like me, so we often hung around each other. This was his fourth combat deployment, and he didn't take any shit. When it came to Fred, though, Dave was a big softy. I'd catch him looking for Fred or calling him over to give him a pet and sneak him a treat.

"Kick that dog again and I'll bury you out here," Dave said, his voice tight but steady.

The Afghan commando wasn't fazed. He'd been looking for some kind of entertainment, and now he had someone's attention.

"He's a filthy, shit dog," he said. "I kick this dog if I want to! Forget you!"

The commando raised his foot again. As he wound up for a second blow, Dave swiftly brought his own foot up, kicking the sole of his boot directly into the commando's chest. The commando flew backward and landed in a heap of dust.

By now a crowd was forming. As the other ANA guys walked over, I was shocked to see their AK-47s in their arms. The commando got up, and the group stood around him, holding their guns.

Across from them, the RECON guys picked up their M4s and stood on the other side, shirtless in their green silkies and flip-flops. I got to my feet and looked around at the marines. Our beards were caked in dirt and our skin had turned brown from the sun and the dust. We looked emaciated. Living off MREs and in a constant state of low-grade anxiety, we'd all dropped ten, fifteen pounds easy. We were angry. Exhausted.

Then I looked down at Fred, who was at Dave's heels. He stood there, panting in the heat, his tail tucked down, confused.

The commando brushed himself off and looked from Dave to Fred. With a rancor that knocked the air from my lungs, he said, "I'm going to shoot this fucking dog," and reached out for a gun from the hands of the guy next to him.

CHAPTER 7

To the Canyon

Here's the thing: there's no manual on how to come home from war. When I first got back from my deployment, my command sent me on a weekend-long postdeployment retreat. There would be sessions on how to identify post-traumatic stress, how to work with the VA and get connected with other resources, and all the other how-to stuff you might expect. Only the retreat I got sent to was in Atlanta, Georgia. So when I showed up in Atlanta and started going to the classes and briefs and meetings, all the speakers and organizations at the retreat were, naturally, Atlanta based. In meeting after meeting, the presenter would stand up and say, "Hi, I'm so-and-so from the Atlanta Veterans Affairs office. I'll be your point of contact for your medical appointments and for filing claims." Meanwhile, I was thinking, I live in D.C., so how are you going to help me? It seemed like a big waste of time. Pretty soon I was skipping classes and hanging out at the hotel bar.

There was only one other person in my family with combat experience—my uncle John—so I took a page from his book. As a kid, Uncle John was like a grandfather to me. He had served in World War II and fought in the Battle of the Bulge, where his whole platoon was just about wiped out. For two weeks, John was missing in action, presumed dead. In fact, he was carefully making his way out from behind enemy lines wearing a stolen German trench coat. He escaped, survived, and made it home. According to the story, by the time Uncle John got back to the States, he was nursing a gunshot wound and had a nasty case of trench foot. But he recovered, settled down with my aunt Alma, had a successful career, and made a happy life for himself and his family in the D.C. area.

The message was simple: you come home and you move on. That's what I planned to do, too, and for a while, it worked. Coming back to my hometown made it easy. I started hanging out with my high school buddies again and reunited with my girlfriend. I worked. I didn't talk much about Afghanistan because I didn't have to; I was surrounded by civilians.

I started checking off all the boxes I thought I should. The first one was a job. My former commanding officer, Tom, helped line up a position for me at the Defense Intelligence Agency (DIA), where he also worked. There, I'd be a reports officer, reviewing, editing, and releasing intelligence reports from collectors in the field, guys with jobs similar to the one I'd held in Sangin but with bigger paychecks.

The next box to check was a new car. I'd always driven beat-up trucks, like the hand-me-down Jeep Wrangler I got from my sister after I graduated boot camp. My friends used to love to tease me about that car, which had a vanity plate that read WLDFLWR from when it was Sarah's. After boot camp, when I was stationed in Charleston and started getting my first real paychecks, I put some work into Wildflower to give her more of an edge: mud tires, a three-inch lift, and a winch on the front. To my friends, though, she would always be Wildflower.

When I finally sold the Jeep, I got an '88 Toyota 4Runner, and later, an '85 Toyota pickup, bright red with a gray interior. I loved that truck. I drove it throughout intelligence training and school, but then the engine died right before I left for my deployment. I wanted to fix her up when I got home, but my dad didn't want me to leave the truck in his garage, and my girl-friend didn't want anything to do with it, either. She hated how it rode rough and that the A/C never worked. So with nowhere to keep the truck, I ended up selling it for next to nothing to a local shop. I was heartbroken.

Once I got back, I felt pressure to avoid getting another "money pit," as my dad and girlfriend liked to call my old trucks. So I bought a brand-new Toyota Tacoma. It had a shiny fresh coat of maroon paint, four doors, and the off-road pack-age. When I drove it off the lot, it was gleamingly perfect, but it wasn't me. It came with a hefty monthly payment, too, and insurance costs like I'd never seen. But I tried to tell myself it was time to grow up and be practical.

Next box: getting serious about my relationship. Through most of my training and later through my deployment, I had the same girlfriend. We knew each other from home, where we'd gone to different high schools with mutual friends. When I got back, we found an apartment and moved in together.

I felt like I should propose, so I planned a vacation for us in Puerto Rico the week before I started the DIA job. We went to one of those cheesy resorts that felt like it could have been anywhere. We ate American food, drank Coke and fruity cocktails, and lounged by the pool. I proposed in the hotel lobby. I planned it so the staff knew ahead of time, and they all came down and stood in a big circle around us. When she said yes, everyone clapped. Upstairs, I had our room filled with flowers and bottles of champagne as a surprise. She went straight to the balcony, though, without seeming to notice, then lit a cigarette and texted pictures of the ring to her friends. I sat at the edge of the bed and watched the smoke rise from her profile in the lounge chair.

And so, within a few months of being home, I'd checked all the boxes I was supposed to check: I had a new car, a new job, a new apartment, and a fiancée. I had done it; I had moved on.

Then summer came around. In D.C., everything was vibrant, green and lush, and in the mornings, you could see the heat rising off the asphalt. People walked around carrying towels over their shoulders, wiping their foreheads on their way to the metro.

In our small apartment, my fiancée had a dog of her own—a little pug whose company Fred didn't particularly enjoy. The worst moments came at mealtimes, when Fred would lie at my feet. The pug would come over to the table, hoping to be handed a morsel of food, but Fred would flip out when he got close, barking and chasing him into the other room. The tension between the two dogs added to tension that was also growing between my fiancée and me.

At the new job, the work was far from glamorous. I had high hopes the position would lead to something bigger—eventually, I thought I could become a case officer, managing intelligence operations with an impact at the national level. But at the start,

I was sitting all day in a cubicle, in front of a computer, reviewing reports. Most of the intelligence coming through was insignificant and obscure. I started realizing many of the reports were essentially generated to meet a quota. The guys in the field were under pressure from their command to produce a certain number, so they wrote up whatever they had, even if it barely qualified as intelligence in the first place. I was frustrated but tried to remain optimistic.

For the Fourth of July that year, I went down to Hilton Head, South Carolina, where my mom lived with my stepdad, Maurice. They had a beautiful home with a big backyard and a deck overlooking a lagoon. After lunch, a few of us sat out back on the patio having a beer. I was joking around with my brother-in-law Jason and my friend Nathan when suddenly the kids next door started launching firecrackers into the lagoon. My body responded before my mind did. In an instant, I grabbed Nathan, who was sitting next to me, and pulled him down. We hit the deck before I realized what I was doing.

"Wow, man," Nathan said. My brother-in-law jumped up and came around to our side of the table.

"I'm sorry," I said, trying to come back to my senses. My heart was racing. The firecrackers were still going off; the *whoosh* sound they made as they flew through the air sounded exactly like RPGs—something I hadn't heard in months. I got to my feet and helped Nathan up, my palms sweating.

"I don't know what happened," I said, trying to smile and brush it off. "I thought the Taliban moved in next door."

Up until that moment, I thought I was in control of my memories and experiences, not that they had any control over me.

That fall, my fiancée suggested we buy a house. Her friends were all moving to the suburbs and starting families. She wanted that, too, but I desperately wanted to live in the city. I was just twenty-eight years old and had spent the last eight years—nearly all of my twenties—in the marines. I tried to convince her the suburbs could wait. If we bought a place in D.C., I argued, we could live there for a few years, enjoy it, then rent it out later, use it as an investment.

She wouldn't budge. I found myself far from the city, looking at three-bedroom houses with two-car garages and big lawns that were right at the top of our budget. I remember standing in the foyer of one house, looking around at the slick hardwood floors and empty rooms, and suddenly everything came crashing into focus. I didn't like what I saw. This wasn't me. I wasn't happy—not with the truck or the house or the job or the person I was supposed to be marrying. I thought checking all the boxes would lead me to where I was supposed to be, but standing in the foyer that day, all I wanted to do was run.

Our arrival in the Kisatchie National Forest was unceremonious. The park entrance had no gate, ranger station, or welcome center. Instead, Josh, Fred, and I were greeted by the quiet of the forest. If there had been any breeze whatsoever, the tall longleaf pines might have waved hello. But the afternoon was hot, humid, and still.

After our night at Red's Lounge in Clarksdale, we'd followed the winding Mississippi River south, down into Louisiana, in hopes of camping in the Kisatchie woods. Kisatchie is a nine-hundred-square-mile swath of central Louisiana, a big green expanse on the map, full of bayous, bogs, prairies, and woods. Safe to say we chose the destination because neither of us had ever heard of it, and no one had recommended it, either.

On the drive down, we'd passed marshes and crossed over narrow muddy deltas until the flat swampland began to give way to stretches of towering pines, making us grateful for shelter from the scorching midafternoon sun.

Inside the park, we spotted a stack of maps in a plastic dispenser hung from a lonely wooden sign. I pulled over and grabbed one, then unfolded the glossy paper across the dash.

"Wow. This place is *huge*," Josh said, taking in the enormous gridded network of trails.

Without studying it too much, I shifted the Land Cruiser back into gear.

We drove for a while before spotting a turnoff. A little plaque with a four-wheel-drive sign marked its entrance. Josh and I looked at each other. I raised my eyebrows, then turned the wheel and pulled onto the trail. I hadn't tested the Land Cruiser's four-wheel-drive system yet, but I knew my big blue beauty was more than capable. This was exactly the sort of road-less-traveled we were after.

There's nothing like the feeling of tires treading over dirt. Josh and I grinned from ear to ear as we bounced over the bumpy trail. The truck steadily moved forward, rocking back and forth as she crawled forward over shallow ditches and bumps. The trail was overgrown, and foliage from the forest floor reached across our path like outstretched arms. Fred, jarred from the rocking, stood looking out the window. The view was a blur of green.

I could feel the dirt beneath us soften, and the road began to tilt forward, downhill. As we came around a bend, the Land Cruiser's bumper pushing through shrubs, the smell of wet earth filtered through the open windows. Ahead, I spotted the source: the road sloped down, right into a fifteen-yard-long stretch of thick, dark Louisiana mud.

We rolled to a stop and I hopped out to look for a twig. Making my way along the edge of the mud pit, I leaned out over it and stuck a long stick down as far as it'd go. When I pulled it out, the watermark looked about two feet deep. I held it up so Josh could see.

"I think we can make it," I said, walking back to the truck. Fred had jumped into the driver's seat and put his head out the window, watching me. Josh hung out the other side. He shrugged.

"We probably can," he said, "but where are we going to make it to, exactly?"

We consulted the park map, but our trail wasn't on it. Wherever we were, we were alone in the thick of the woods, with no cell phone service and no plan.

I hopped back in the driver's seat and nudged Fred out of the way.

"Your call, man," Josh said.

Fred stuck his head out the window behind me. I could see the reflection of his goofy smile in the side-view mirror.

"Let's do it," I said. I shifted the old LC into four-wheel drive and eased us forward. If we went slowly enough, I hoped we'd have enough torque to get through the slop.

The front wheels went in first, and we tipped forward as the nose of the truck pushed into the watery mud. The Cruiser righted herself and pulled her rear tires in. As the back wheels rolled into the mud, though, I felt the entire weight of the truck sink. The tires slipped, and we lost traction. I pressed my right foot harder onto the gas, but that just sent mud flying up from all four tires. Only five feet into our mud pit and we were stuck. I glanced at Josh, who looked at me as if to say I'd better have a plan.

For a moment, we just sat there. I felt a cool prick of anxiety start at the back of my neck and flush through my body. Then I gripped the small shifter on my right and pulled it straight back into the lowest gear we had.

I returned my foot to the gas and slowly pressed down. Beneath us, I felt the power shift through the Land Cruiser, and she lurched forward. Josh sat up in his seat and pounded the outside of the passenger side door. Fred stood from the backseat with his head between us, trying to get a view of the action.

"Come on, baby! Keep rollin'!" Josh shouted, and she did. The mud sloshed along the bottom of the doors and we slowly glided forward. When we crawled out of the pit on the other side, we headed uphill again, victorious.

Thankfully, the overgrown trail dumped us onto a well-maintained fire road, and, after another mile, we came to a campground. It'd been nearly ten hours in the car, and we were finished pushing our luck. We drove into the campground and had our pick of a site; no one else was around. I parked the Cruiser between two enormous pine trees and we got out.

It was a relief to stand and stretch. Fred leapt out behind us onto the piney forest floor and got to work examining the area.

The humidity hadn't eased up at all, and mosquitoes immediately descended onto our bare arms and legs. Josh and I set out to look for kindling and logs to burn. The sooner we got a fire going, the quicker we could stave off the bugs.

We found a narrow trail into the woods. The dense canopy obscured much of what was left of the daylight, but still, it was hot, and I wiped the sweat from my forehead. Back in the truck, our cooler was packed with meat, veggies, and beer. Josh had brought a cast-iron skillet, perfect for using over an open flame.

A soft layer of pine needles lined the flat, compressed earth of the trail. I walked along, picking up a few sticks and twigs. Then, I caught sight of a small, innocuous thing: a small stack of rocks just ahead, right in my path. A lightning bolt of thought flickered in my mind: *Don't step there.*

I'd noticed rock stacks like this before, on hikes with Fred in Virginia. Hikers or campers would make a little pile of stones, one balanced on top of the other, small sculptures that served little purpose other than to mark a trail and pass the time. Cairns, they're called. For anyone who had patrolled in Afghanistan, however, the rocks served a completely different purpose. The Taliban often stacked rocks as a way of signaling to one another and to villagers the location of IEDs. We had been trained to spot such formations and to be cautious of them.

Rocks weren't the only thing the Taliban used to mark IEDs. Trash was common, too. A wrapper. A soda can. Anything shiny or out of place that we might instinctively grab or kick. Before my mission in Sangin, a unit of marines took up post in an abandoned compound near the Green Zone. The corpsman caught sight of a box of tampons lying in the dirt. Maybe out of boredom, or amusement, or just to clear it away, he kicked it. It was attached to an IED and blew him up. He lived, but the blast took three of his limbs. That's what gave rise to our "pattern of life" rule. After that, we only ever took compounds where people were living, and even still, the EOD guys would sweep for IEDs before we moved in. Even in places that were inhabited, sometimes we'd still find IEDs that remained.

The feeling of living like that—in what was essentially a minefield—didn't leave you when you got home. After I first came back from my deployment, I'd catch myself avoiding pieces of trash or rocks as I walked down the sidewalk or through a park. The sound of a garbage truck lumbering down the street and suddenly hitting a pothole, or a plane flying low overhead, sometimes made me duck, too. And driving around in D.C., I instinctively watched pedestrians on either side of the road. Instead of my mind registering that some guy was simply out for his morning jog, it'd ask: *What time is it? Why is he out jogging? Have I seen him before?*

On the trail in Kisatchie, a jolt of adrenaline washed through me like a wave, then passed. In an instant, I registered that I was home now, that a rock was just a rock again, that it had been stripped of its danger now. I took a breath, looked up, and there was Fred, gleefully bounding through the brush off to our right. I watched him hop over a log and sniff along the bottom of a tree trunk. He lifted his chin up, twitching his wet nose and scanning the horizon. When his eyes landed on Josh and the bundle of sticks he was carrying, he trotted toward him and, with a quick leap, snatched a twig from under his arm.

"Hey!" Josh said, playfully, then pretended to chase Fred, who held the long, thin stick between his teeth, letting Josh come just close enough before dashing away.

Back at camp, Josh and I started the fire while Fred gnawed contentedly on his stolen twig, propping it up between his front paws while he reduced it to a slobbery nub. Stunningly, the cooler had managed to keep our food and drinks cold in the back of the truck all day, and it wasn't long before we were sipping beer and flipping steaks. When the sun went down, the heat stayed, but the bugs were gone and our bellies were full.

That night in my tent, I tossed and turned. Fred splayed out in one corner while I lay across my sleeping mat, waking up every hour to wipe the sweat from my forehead and reposition. Sometime around 3:00 A.M., I awoke to shuffling and crackling sounds outside the tent. I propped myself up on an elbow and looked over at Fred, who was already awake, twitching his nose in the air. I leaned toward the flap of the tent, slowly pulling the zipper down. Outside was a whole pack of wild hogs roaming through the campsite, including an enormous one right outside our tent. They were hulking creatures, snorting and honking over the ground, looking for food. Fred, now fully alert, started growling. "Easy, buddy," I said, and he came over and curled up next to me. The noisy intruders moved on, and we managed a few more hours of sleep.

The next morning, Josh and I decided to get back on the road. We'd thought we'd spend a few days camping in Kisatchie, but one restless night in the heat was enough. Even though we were in search of the challenge and uncertainty of being off the grid—the feeling of the day-to-day grind and immediacy of life in Afghanistan—the bayou had put us in our place. It was a contradiction: we wanted to be back in Afghanistan, but then again, we didn't. Maybe it would always be that way.

After our night in Kisatchie, the bungalow we'd rented in Austin sounded pretty good. We drove out of the park, dark red mud flinging off the Land Cruiser's tires as we merged onto the paved highway leading us out. In Austin, we spent a weekend sleeping on real beds, eating from food trucks, and relaxing on the banks of Barton Creek. Refreshed, we struck out on the road again, heading northwest toward our first big destination of the trip: the Grand Canyon. Neither of us had seen it before, and we were excited. We planned to spend a night with a friend of Josh's in Santa Fe before pushing onward into Arizona. The driving days would be long: over ten hours to New Mexico and at least six more to the canyon. But we were hitting our stride. We'd been on the road now for almost two weeks, and we were falling into a rhythm. I stubbornly insisted on doing most of the driving, leaving Josh in charge of the music and Fred in charge of sleeping. We branched out from Johnny Cash and listened to my favorites—Huey Lewis and the News, Sturgill Simpson, and eighties hits from my favorite movies, *Ferris Bueller's Day Off* and *Back to the Future*—along with Josh's favorites, Smashing Pumpkins, Pearl Jam, and the Red Hot Chili Peppers.

Driving across central Texas, the temperature spiked to nearly one hundred degrees again, and the Land Cruiser rose and fell over narrow roads that cut through the sloping plains. The open expanse was endless, interrupted every so often by skeletal oil pumps that sat slumped toward the earth. On the horizon, rock formations reached into the sky and hung in the distance like planets. It felt like we were in a Road Runner and Wile E. Coyote cartoon.

In need of gas, we pulled into a big Mobil station, sun scorched and faded, in a run-down refinery town. Behind the low building, trailer homes were lined up in the sun and a few shoeless kids ran around kicking a half-deflated soccer ball. A couple of mean-looking stray dogs paced back and forth, panting in the heat. I decided to leave Fred in the truck. Inside, I picked up a huge bag of beef jerky for five bucks, and with a full tank of gas, we continued on to Santa Fe and, from there, to the Grand Canyon.

Unlike Kisatchie, which was empty, the Grand Canyon was an ordeal. The road leading to the entrance was thick with RVs, campers, minivans, and tourists with hats and hiking boots. When we pulled up to the ranger's gate, in the middle of the afternoon, a young woman with dark hair and a smile kindly delivered some sobering news: all campsites in the park were booked up for weeks. Instead, she pointed us in the direction we came from, toward overflow campsites outside the park. We drove a few minutes to the campsite and decided to relax there for the rest of the afternoon instead of struggling through the tourists and the heat. We'd be the first ones at the gate the next morning to snap some pictures, then be on our way.

We found a tucked-away spot with a big picnic table and fire ring—just the right amount of luxury. Josh and I made a small fire and cracked open a few PBRs. Fred stretched out across the dirt, and we stared into the flames together.

Josh and I had picked up fresh steak and veggies from a nearby market; hungry for dinner, we cooked them up over the fire. I fetched Fred's bowl out of the truck, and after filling it with kibble, added a few nice pieces of steak for him, too. When I set the bowl down in front of him, though, he hesitated. Instead of eating, he nudged his nose into the earth and pushed dirt and pine needles into the bowl, covering his food. It gave me chills to see it. I thought of his little pile of scraps under the bushes by the burn pit in Afghanistan, the place where he went to hide any food that he found around the compound. When we were camping like this—exposed, out in the open—I wondered if it brought Fred back to Sangin.

Often, the two of us were affected by the same triggers— big crowds and loud noises, like fireworks or a car backfiring. One time, back home in D.C., Fred and I were walking to the local farmers' market when a truck came barreling down the street. It felt like the sidewalk beneath us was vibrating. Fred got spooked and pulled on the leash, trying to get away. I bent down and scooped him up, carrying him in my arms the last block to the market. "It's okay, buddy," I said. Another time, the smoke detector went off in the middle of the night in our apartment. Fred, who had been sleeping on the floor somewhere, leapt into bed. Even after I got up and replaced the batteries and got the loud, incessant chirping to stop, Fred lay next to me shaking. It was the way he reacted to fireworks, too. I pulled the rattled dog close to me and held him until we both fell back to sleep.

In the campground, I watched as Fred buried his food instead of enjoying it, his survival instincts kicking in yet again. I knew he was hungry but that he would ignore his hunger if he didn't feel that it was safe to eat. The only thing I could do was sit with him. I grabbed the bowl and pulled out some of the pine needles and chunks of dirt. I sat down next to him, took a sip of my beer, and looked out into the distance. I waited like that, without looking down, until I heard him crunching on bits of kibble. He worked through most of his meal like that, with me sitting there silently, letting him know he was safe. In moments like that, we took turns reminding each other that we were no longer in a combat zone—that we were going to be okay.

The sky turned yellow and orange, then a deep royal blue, then dark. We spent the rest of the night looking into the fire, all in agreement that a properly burning fire was better than cable. Overhead, stars began to blink through the inky night. Turning my face up in admiration, I caught a few shooting across the sky, brilliant dashes of glittering white light.

At dawn, the air was cool and crisp. I unzipped my tent and, shivering, made my way to the Land Cruiser for my Jetboil. Fred scampered out behind me, shook, and looked around. He trotted over to the brush and sniffed his way to a spot he deemed worthy of marking. Josh emerged from his tent, too, and we quickly got to work breaking down camp. We wanted to get our view of the canyon before the tourists and RV folks had even finished brushing their teeth.

We easily made it through the gate before any crowds had formed, and as the mist rose up out of the canyon, the three of us were cruising Desert View Drive to a lookout on the South Rim. On either side of the road, the green brush grew high toward the sky, obscuring our view.

As we came slowly around a bend, I moved my foot to the

brake. Ahead of us was a herd of enormous mule deer—as tall as the truck and built thick, like cows. They swiveled their heads toward us, blinking their big brown eyes, then nonchalantly continued across the road toward the brush. Fred stuck his snout out the window cautiously, twitching his nose, huffing and growling in low, quiet bursts.

"What's wrong, buddy?" I said. "Little bigger than the deer back home, huh?"

Josh and I laughed. Fred loved to chase deer on trail runs in parks outside D.C., and typically, he'd be hanging out the window bellowing and barking like a maniac. He must've been able to tell these deer were a different kind of beast.

We continued down the winding road, and after a few minutes the brush began to thin and a breeze streamed through our open windows. Nearing the canyon's edge, we arrived at the turnoff for our overlook, parked, and jumped out. Next to an old observation tower, we found the mouth of a trail and headed down. I broke into a run, and Josh and Fred followed.

Nothing can prepare you for a view like that. Even calling it a "view" is an oversimplification. The canyon looked unreal, like a painting. Layers of brown, red, orange, and black stretched on in gradients against the bright, cloudless sky. The depth and expanse were dizzying—incomprehensible. The three of us stood in silence for what would have otherwise been an uncomfortable amount of time, quietly looking into the distance as the wind rose up and wafted over us in gentle gusts.

We took a few pictures—some of Josh standing triumphantly with his hands on his hips and a few with him holding his leg above his head. When it was my turn, I scooped Fred up and propped him across my shoulders. We both smiled for the camera, the mighty Colorado River and massive canyon at our backs.

Afterward, taking one last look at the endless formations of rock, I couldn't help but feel insignificant. I thought about how all those layers in the canyon walls represented the passage of time—all the ages that came before us and would come after us. All the lives and stories of people who passed through here, and all the many who never would. I knew our story was just one. Yet, standing there with my dog and my friend—two beings I never would have met had my life gone another way—I was in awe of the profound unlikelihood and beauty of it all.

CHAPTER 8

Extract

The RECON marines and ANA commandos stood across from each other, sweaty and grimacing in the sun, guns in their arms. Fred cowered at Dave's feet.

"Stand the fuck down," Jason, the royal marine in charge of the ANA group, said, stepping right into the middle of the group. "Drop your weapons," he growled to the Afghan commandos, "or you can expect your pay to be withheld."

The threat of docked pay defused the situation quickly. Jason walked right up to the commando who had kicked Fred and, for good measure, grabbed the AK-47 from his hands. With that, he and the rest of the commandos shuffled through the dust back to their side of the compound and I followed a few of the marines into the command center, Fred at my heels.

The atmosphere in the compound was uneasy, to say the least. The fact that we had gotten anywhere close to engaging in a gunfight with the commandos was unacceptable. We were nearing the end of our mission, and all nerves were shot. We looked and felt like crap. Trekking for miles each night through canals and cornfields and ditches, never knowing if the next step would be your last, was wearing on all of us. But there was also something off about the commando who had kicked Fred. We'd all heard chilling stories about green-on-blue attacks—where Afghan forces attacked coalition forces—and we were unnerved by his behavior.

We squatted down on dusty mats and orange-stained pillows in the command center, sweating. Someone passed around vacuum-sealed fudge brownies.

"We need to come up with a Fred watch," Jason said. "We need to agree that we'll be accountable for him, especially at night. We gotta keep him away from the commandos—if he bothers them or gets in their way, it might force their hand." The commandos had a room at the other side of the compound where they slept. We didn't want Fred wandering over there while we were out on patrols. We all agreed to keep a closer watch on the dog, especially Top, who was usually with Fred all night while we were patrolling.

But what was really on our minds was a much bigger question: What would become of Fred when we left? We were extracting soon, in about a week, the same way we'd come in: by helicopter in the middle of the night. No one wanted to leave Fred behind. He'd become one of us. For the past three weeks, he'd lived in the dirt with us, patrolled with us, comforted us, and given us something to smile about, without asking anything in return. He wasn't like other strays in Sangin. I couldn't picture him joining a pack of those huge howling dogs, roaming through the Green Zone at night, barking and fighting over food. And after witnessing Fred getting kicked, the threat of human cruelty loomed in my mind, too.

While all the RECON guys had grown attached to Fred,

responsibility for him fell at my feet. All the guys knew—and I knew, too—that Fred was my dog. He followed me around, slept on my mat, and kept an eye on me more than anyone else. I knew we had a special bond from the moment I handed him a piece of jerky that first day. So as the final days of our mission slipped by, the pressure mounted for me to figure out a plan to get Fred out.

The challenge was threefold. First, there was the issue of sneaking the dog onto the helicopter and smuggling him back to Camp Leatherneck. Second, once we were back, I'd have to figure out a way to ship him halfway around the globe back to the States—a huge logistical challenge I didn't even know how to begin to tackle. And third, while I was figuring out how to get Fred to the U.S., I'd need to somehow keep him concealed on Leatherneck, a place where, if caught, he'd be put down immediately.

Having Fred at Leatherneck was what worried me the most. Leatherneck was huge, like the Pentagon of Helmand Province—home to the largest number of coalition troops in-country. And many of the marines were high ranking, with nothing better to do than narc on the sergeant with a dog in his room. I'd only spent a few weeks at Leatherneck—before and after my Trek Nawa mission—and I'd already seen how much our every move was scrutinized, how easy it was to get into trouble. One night in the chow hall, as I walked back to my table with a tray of lasagna (with an extra scoop of watery "meat" sauce), I got ambushed by a first sergeant.

"What's on your face, asshole?" he said, leaning into me before continuing with a string of expletives. It was a mustache—

technically, one within regulation, but clearly not to this guy's liking. I went to the barracks and shaved it off.

Another time, the problem was my wearing my watch cap on base (the military-issue tan beanies are only supposed to be used in the field), and another time the concern was a non-issue green shirt under my cammies.

They were small, stupid moments of "discipline" from bored and frustrated leaders, but that was the environment on base. I could only imagine the more extreme consequences I'd face if I got caught with a dog—anything from removal from operations to time in the brig. Everyone knew there was a nationwide order from the commanding general of all U.S. forces in Afghanistan: no pets. Worse, if we got caught, Fred would be euthanized immediately, no questions asked. I would have effectively killed him by removing him from his natural environment. How could I risk that? Instead of endangering both of our lives, I wondered if I should just snap some pictures of my furry friend and keep them as a pleasant memory.

Around the compound, the guys worked on me. Plenty of them had stories. "I heard about a guy in Iraq who used this organization called Baghdad Pups," said Will, a civil affairs attachment. Someone else thought he had heard of a local SPCA back home that raised money to get dogs out. Those were nice suggestions, but we didn't have that kind of time. Plus, in every other dog story I'd ever heard, the dog in question had been hanging around a base for months, coming by for food, and eventually, over time, someone took the initiative on figuring out the paperwork to get the dog out. In our case, we were *taking* Fred from the compound where we found him—against orders—and bringing him to a place where you'd get your ass handed to you if you didn't have a proper shave.

Matt and Dave, the EOD guys I spent a lot of time with, were adamant. "We'll keep him at the EOD compound," Matt said. On Leatherneck, the EOD unit had their own section of the base, relatively removed. "It'll be fine," Dave said. "We'll figure it out."

Since Top was in leadership, he couldn't promise anything. But he did say he'd pass around a hat back on base and round up donations to go toward the cost of shipping Fred home.

"You're gonna figure it out," the guys would say. "You can do it, Grossi."

I knew the guys meant what they said. I knew they'd help me. But I also took their promises with a grain of salt. Back on base, everyone goes back to their own lives. People spend their time calling home, hitting the gym, doing office work, reconnecting with buddies. We'd all be going our separate ways for a while, taking space, resting. Anyone looking after Fred would not only have to deal with the hassle of hiding him, but they'd be putting their career on the line. I trusted the guys, but I also knew someone had to take responsibility for Fred, and that was me. *If I do this,* I thought, *I'm on my own.*

As the sun went down on extraction day, the marines on the rooftop positions pulled out their knives and slashed through the sandbags in front of them. The bags sagged, weeping sand and dust. Down below, under the glow of red lights, we rolled up our sleeping mats and bug nets, collected our grenades and magazine rounds, rounded up our iPods and beat-up copies of *Car and Driver,* and condensed everything into our rucks. The burn pit, which was always sort of smoldering, consumed the last of our MRE wrappers and shit. We threw in the dead batteries that had powered our radios and laptops; they cracked and popped in the heat, sending splinters of plastic into the air. The black smoke billowed into the sky. As long as the wind was in your favor, you could almost avoid the stench. But if you breathed it in, you could never really breathe it out.

Bringing a helicopter down in a combat zone is a huge risk. One well-placed RPG round and boom—there goes the whole platoon. Extracting was going to be one of the most vulnerable points in our mission. There was no way we could do it from our current compound. The Taliban knew exactly where we were, and we were too close to the Green Zone. The plan was to dismantle our makeshift base in the middle of the night, hump to a compound a few miles away—into the desert, farther from the Green Zone—and get picked up in the dark, undetected.

Earlier that day, while gathering up my belongings, I spent some quality time with Fred. I gave him his favorite beef jerky and the dusty old rope he loved to play tug-of-war with. I'd already taken a bunch of pictures of him, but I realized I didn't have any of us together. Before I packed up my camera, I handed it to one of the guys and hoisted Fred onto my lap for a photo. In the picture, my face is turned toward the shutter but Fred's looking at the rope in my hand, his front paws reaching toward it. You can see the tip of his pink tongue hanging from his snout and the goofy expression of a puppy focused on his favorite toy. After the photo was taken, we played a little longer, and I scratched him behind the ears and massaged his neck. It was as close to a good-bye as I'd let myself get.

I still wasn't convinced about bringing Fred back to Leatherneck. I knew I wanted to bring the dog home, but I could only rationalize taking the risk if I felt certain that Fred wanted to come, too. If he seemed content staying in his compound—the only home he'd known—then I'd accept it as the best thing for him.

With all of us working in the moonlight, it didn't take long before the compound returned more or less to the state we'd found it in—festering burn pit and holes in the walls notwithstanding. Nothing else was left behind. Our makeshift home would soon be crawling with Taliban, and we made sure we didn't leave anything they could use.

Loaded up with our gear, we lined up by the back door. I thought I saw Fred poking around the burn pit looking for scraps. The guys got quiet as we got ready to head out, and I focused on the journey ahead. When the first marine pushed through the doorway, we followed him into the night, single file, the same way we'd come.

The desert was cool and clear, with a sliver of moon overhead. Through my night vision, I looked out at the open landscape of sloping sand hills rolling softly into the distance. The wide expanse was a welcome change from the dense cornfields and network of canals in the Green Zone. Our packs were heavy, but we moved quickly and freely. I felt like I could see for miles in every direction—but I didn't see Fred. I'd wanted him to make the decision for me, and now he had. I told myself I should accept it—it was for the best. But I was heartbroken.

A couple of hours later, miles from our compound, we approached another compound that had been scouted by drone. It was smaller and full of goats—a good sign there wasn't a network of IEDs underfoot. We filed in, and a few RECON guys made a rooftop position to scout from. Other than that, we kept a low profile. Morning was close. Once light broke, we'd spend the day waiting for dark to return and, with it, our ride out of there.

For the first time in weeks, I felt the weight of the mission begin to lift. I didn't have any reports to write. There were no villagers to talk to. We were getting out—and we were getting out with all our guys, no less. That felt like nothing short of a miracle, given what we had expected from Sangin. The bullet that passed through Joe's helmet had been the closest we had come to losing a guy. We were lucky. Now, we could rest. As the morning sun began to peek up over the horizon, I sat down and leaned back onto my ruck, finally allowing myself to think about my upcoming hot shower and hot meal rather than how much I would miss Fred. I stretched my legs out in front of me and crossed my arms on my chest, nodding my head back against the wall and closing my eyes.

I awoke to shouts from the guys on the roof.

"Grossi! Get up here!"

Daylight had broken across the new compound. I blinked my eyes open and saw the guys lying and sitting in the shade along the perimeter walls. Disoriented, I got to my feet. I looked over to where the shouts came from and made my way to the post. A rickety wooden ladder leaned against the clay shelter, and I climbed up, crawling next to the guys. Someone handed me binoculars.

"Look who it is," he said.

The desert, glowing and hazy in the morning sun, looked almost out of focus. There were miles of nothing and then, coming toward us, a squatty white dog trailed by a cloud of dust. Goosebumps rose on my arms. It was Fred, the sun in his eyes, bounding toward us with that signature bounce in his step, chin up.

"Dude must've needed to pack!" The guys laughed.

I blinked away the sting of tears. I couldn't believe it.

"Good boy," I whispered.

Fred pranced right through the doorway of the compound like he owned the place. In typical Fred fashion, he greeted each marine one at a time, howling and *woo-wooing*, dancing between us with joy. I came down from the roof and grabbed a piece of beef jerky. When Fred frolicked over to me, I swear he was smiling. He wound through my legs in excitement, as if to say, "Where'd you go?" I squatted down to give him the jerky, then pulled out my collapsible coffee cup and poured him some water. As he lapped it up, I shook my head in disbelief. Had he spent the night scavenging through the burn pit? Was he waiting for the sun to come up before making his trek? I'm not sure how he did it, but Fred had tracked us down.

After sunrise, the temperature spiked, as it always did. Fred, entertained by the goats, chased them from one corner of the compound to another. He trotted over, lowering his head to the ground to nip at their wobbly ankles, and they squealed and dashed away as he followed. The guys and I sat around in the shade watching and laughing. We were still stunned and excited that Fred had followed us. But if I was going to get him out of the field completely, there was still the issue of how, exactly, I'd get him on the bird.

We talked about it for what felt like hours, strategizing ways to pull it off.

"What if we just walk him onto the helicopter like he's a working dog?" Jason suggested. Back at the compound, Jason had woven together some paracord, using a button from his trousers to fasten it around Fred's neck with the leftover cord as a leash. Fred had hated the thing and managed to wriggle free each time we put it on him. Jason still had the paracord, but the plan didn't make sense to me.

"There's no way we'll get away with that, man," I said. "They know we didn't come here with a dog—we can't just stroll onto the helicopter with one when we leave."

"What if we just hide Fred in our gear?" someone suggested. In the field, we all carried thin, foldable duffel bags; if a fellow marine was injured in action, you'd use the bag to gather the guy's equipment so nothing got left behind. We got out a duffel bag and tried to see how Fred would react to being put inside it. Unsurprisingly, it was a no-go. Two guys held the bag open while I lifted Fred by the torso and placed him down. As soon as he hit the ground, he threw his head back, squirmed relentlessly, and bolted off. Tail wagging, he sauntered back and stood there looking at us, as if to say, "Try it again!" He thought it was a game.

Jim, the corpsman who had helped remove Fred's bugs, had a slightly better idea.

"I can give him Benadryl. It'll knock him out, then you can put him right in and he won't know the difference."

I figured it was worth a shot. Jim stuck the little pink pill on the back of Fred's tongue and closed his hands around his snout till he swallowed. Fred settled down and closed his eyes, but it was hard to tell if it was the Benadryl or if Fred just got tired and decided to take a nap. We sat in the shade, Fred sleeping next to me, and the guys took turns coming over to ask if I had a plan or to tell me to "just do it." "Grossi, you gotta do it, man," they pressed. Fed up with the pressure mounting, I told them to fuck off. "Relax. I'm working on it," I said.

It wasn't long before Fred was up and moseying around the compound again. With the marines off my back for a minute, I decided to make a deal with Fred. Gently, I pulled him toward me.

"Okay, buddy," I said, looking into his light brown eyes. "If you really want to get out of here, you're gonna have to show me one more thing. Okay?"

I told myself, and I told Fred, that if he followed me toward the helicopter when it came—if he wasn't afraid of the noise and the dust—then I'd do it. I'd take him with me. The whole undertaking still wracked me with anxiety—I didn't want to feel like I was stealing this dog, and I didn't want to put him or anyone else in danger. To go through with it, I needed one last sign.

I stuffed my duffel bag into my cargo pocket so it'd be easy to reach. If the time came, one way or another, I'd get Fred inside.

I started making calls with my sat phone. I was close with my commanding officer, Gomez, back at Leatherneck. He managed me and about six other intel guys doing similar jobs, so I knew he was busy. I also trusted him. I liked the fact that he didn't micromanage me. He was a good boss. I decided to call him and feel him out.

With our extract just hours away, I got to the point.

"Gomez, I might be bringing a dog back with me," I told him.

I don't remember if he laughed or sighed. But he was pretty clear in his response: "I'm not gonna tell you you can't," he said. "But if you get caught, you're on your own."

It was probably the best I could have hoped for, given the circumstances. I asked Gomez to pass the phone to Sergio, an analyst we worked with and one of my close buddies at Leatherneck. Sergio was a smart, fast-talking Puerto Rican–Italian guy who wore big thick glasses. We called him the Tactical Rain Man because he seemed to see numbers everywhere and speak in math. He was the kind of person who was so smart that he had trouble communicating with the rest of us—we couldn't keep up. Without knowing where he was going, he'd start down a sentence, then stop and say it a different way, barely stopping to take a breath. For as much as we teased him about his verbal similarity to Porky Pig, he had the biggest heart of anyone I'd met in the marines. I knew I could trust Sergio to help me.

On Leatherneck, we were lucky enough to have a few Toyota HiLux pickup trucks at our disposal, which we used to get to and from meetings across base. If someone could bring one of those trucks to meet us when we landed, I knew we could whisk Fred away as fast as possible before anyone realized what was going on.

"Hey, man," I said when Sergio came on the line. "I need you and McGuire to bring the truck to the flight line when we land. I might have a dog with me."

Sergio didn't even hesitate before promising to be there with McGuire. McGuire—Mac, we called him—was a radio guy from Wyoming. He was an Iraq veteran and a solid marine with a great sense of humor. He was itching to get out of Leatherneck on a mission, but most of the RECON marines had their own radio operators, so Mac was stuck back at the base in an office with Sergio. It drove him nuts. Eventually he went out on a few missions, but they weren't with me.

Next, I called my big sister, Sarah, back in Virginia. In her work as a special education teacher and school counselor, she'd seen her way around tough situations. But she always kept a cool head and wasn't afraid to take action.

I told her what had happened, about how Fred had followed us and how I was trying to bring him back with me. I also briefed her on the risks and how screwed I'd be if I got caught. Sarah was unfazed and already a step ahead of me. I'd mentioned Fred to Sarah on a call a couple of weeks back; since then, she'd been e-mailing a few organizations to get an idea of how we'd be able to get Fred back to the States and through customs.

"Oh, hush," she told me now. "If anyone can do it, it's you, Craig. If you get him out of the field, I'll take care of the rest."

The calls gave me hope, but they didn't exactly calm my nerves. As the extract time approached, I paced around, checking my gear, checking on Fred, thinking, overthinking. Then we got a call informing us that our extract had been rolled by eight hours. Instead of getting picked up in the darkness of night, the helicopters would come in at daybreak. It was unsettling news. The Taliban had recently shot down a helicopter in the north; if we left in the light of day, what was going to stop the same thing from happening to us? If I was having a tough time getting Fred into the duffel bag, that delay in our departure could be critical. As much as I loved Fred, this wasn't a game, and when it came to it, I knew I wasn't going to risk the lives of marines for the sake of a dog.

I didn't sleep much that night. In the morning, everyone was quiet as we packed up. Three birds were coming in, and I'd be on the first one. We assembled along the wall, and I stood toward the back of the line with Dave and Top. The guys were jittery, shifting from foot to foot. Fred, sensing something was about to happen, bopped around, weaving between our legs and looking up at us with anticipation, tail wagging, eyebrows twitching, just like he used to do when he joined us on patrols. Looking at Fred, I felt a tightness in my chest. This might be it.

The low thump of the rotors in the distance broke the morning quiet. The CH-53 helicopters we used to get in and out of the field were huge—they looked like giant flying coffee cans, as if the barrels of their dull gray bodies defied every law of physics to hover in the air. Two would land and load up first while the third hovered for cover. Once the first two were back in the air, the third would come down for the last of the guys.

As the first giant machine began to descend just outside the compound wall, a wave of sand and dust erupted into the air like a fog. *Shit,* I thought. It was a brownout. When a helicopter flies toward you, it kicks up a wave of dust. That wave washes over you once, then clears. When a helicopter comes in at a different angle, though, descending straight down in a hover instead, the dust comes up and lingers. It makes a relatively simple thing—boarding the helicopter—complicated and dangerous. With poor visibility, marines have been killed in brownouts, accidentally running into tail rotors.

As the rotor wash blanketed us, I caught sight of Fred, who was pacing nervously. Then the line began moving forward. I ducked through the doorway of the compound, following Dave ahead of me, only to be immediately pelted by dust and rocks. I coughed and squinted my eyes, stepping through the brown cloud toward the deafening sound of the whirring rotors. All I could see was Dave's rucksack ahead of me, but no Fred.

Then, I felt a poke at my heel and looked down. Through the grit and grime, there was Fred's face—that long white snout, black nose, and squinting eyes—looking up at me. He was blinking in the dust, barely able to open his eyes. His ears were pinned back and he looked terrified. But there it was. My sign.

I pulled the duffel bag from my cargo pocket. From behind us, Top's hand emerged through the dust and clutched Fred by the scruff. He lifted him like a jug of milk.

"We're doing this!" Top shouted. In one fluid motion, I yanked open the mouth of the bag and Top dropped Fred inside. I zipped it, and we each picked it up by a handle, rushing forward.

A young air winger stood at the back of the chopper, rifle up, scanning the horizon and watching us board. I remember how clean he looked: a washed face, no beard, perfect uniform. I swear I got a whiff of his Axe body spray.

He looked at Top and me, lowered his gaze to the bag between us, and scowled. He reached his arm out to stop us, parting his lips to say something, but Top lifted his forearm, elbow bent, and blocked him.

"Don't worry about it!" he barked, and we stepped up onto the ramp.

We were the last to board. As soon as our feet touched the floor of the chopper, the air winger ducked in behind us, resuming his position at the .50-caliber machine gun on the ramp, and the helicopter lifted back into the air.

I sat on the floor, leaning back into my pack with Fred in the duffel between my legs. The RECON guys all looked at me with huge grins, and Top extended his beer can of a fist for a congratulatory bump.

I pressed my palms onto Fred's back, through the bag, trying to let him know he was okay. I could only imagine what must have been going through his mind. Here was a dog who had never even ridden in a car before, and now he was flying through the air in a helicopter. I felt him squirm, trying to get comfortable, then settle. "Good boy," I whispered.

As we soared through the morning sky, somewhere over Helmand Province, Afghanistan, I realized this scrappy, short-legged, dusty dog was officially mine now. He'd put his trust in me. The real challenge still lay before us, but I was resolved. I knew I'd lie, steal, and cheat to protect Fred. My sister was right: if there was a person to do this, it was me. I'd have to find a way.

CHAPTER 9

California

After my fiancée and I split up, not long after we'd gone house hunting, I moved out and got a studio apartment in the city. It was small, with just enough room for a couch and a bed, but it was all I needed. I stocked the freezer with microwavable burritos and used my woobie—a thin, camouflage-print military-issue blanket—as my bedspread. Every night, Fred curled up between my legs, just as he had in Sangin. We had our bachelor pad, and we were happy.

I sold the shiny new Tacoma and bought a bike. I rode it everywhere, including to work every day. The job continued to be the wrong kind of challenge—I was often bored and felt like I wasn't doing meaningful work—but coming home to Fred afterward was the best part of my day. Our first-floor apartment faced a courtyard, and as I walked through it every night, I'd sneak up on Fred to see what he was doing. Peering through the windows, which were all covered in "Fred tint"—my affectionate term for the snot Fred left on the glass from mashing his snout into it—I'd spot him asleep on the bed, curled up on the woobie. When I opened the door, he'd go nuts. Fred would scurry over to greet me, sliding across the hardwood floor and letting out joyful howls. He'd zip between my legs, then jump back onto the bed, then jump down and race back over. His tail wagged a mile a minute, and his whole body wiggled with glee. There was nothing better. His joy eclipsed my frustration at spending another day in the sausage factory that is our federal government.

Once we were thoroughly reacquainted with one another, I'd get out of my suit and tie as quick as I could, put on my running shoes, and we'd be out the door. We ran every day. I had always wanted to get out of the suburbs where I'd grown up and live in the city. Now that I was finally there, all I wanted to do was soak it up. We had a route: left out of the building, straight down to the Capitol, then a mile down the hill past the Washington Monument to the World War II memorial, then up past the White House and back home. I loved taking in the sights of the city with Fred. It felt like we were jogging through history.

The big problem continued to be work. I felt stuck. While I'd gotten close with my coworkers and loved working alongside them, the days were monotonous, and I didn't feel like my work was making an impact. I started thinking about going back to school. I was in a contract position and my career opportunities seemed limited. If I got my degree, I could come back to the intelligence world as a government employee with more options available to me.

My commanding officer in Afghanistan, Gomez, had gone to Georgetown. For whatever reason, he had always nudged me to apply, even back when we were in Helmand Province. I'm not sure what gave him the confidence in me or in the idea that I should go there, but when I came home, he e-mailed me the contact information of the dean of the School of Continuing Studies.

When it felt like my career at the DIA was stalling out, I remembered that. Georgetown had a prestigious reputation, and I didn't know if I could get in, but I liked the idea of trying. Just as my attraction to the Marine Corps and to the intelligence field had been about being challenged and pushed, I was drawn to Georgetown because I knew it wouldn't be easy. In my experience, marines were commonly told how quickly and easily they could earn a degree once they finished serving. That never sat right with me. Don't get me wrong—I had never been a great student and I was nervous about the idea of going back to school—but if I was going to do it, I wanted to do it right. You can't have it good and fast at the same time; you have to pick one. I figured if I was going to get my degree, I wanted to get it from the best school I could.

I remember writing my application essay about what I'd learned in intelligence and from being a marine. I enjoyed writing it. As a kid, I was drawn to storytelling. At work, I wrote plenty, but it'd been ages since I did any creative writing, and I remembered how good it felt.

In the spring of 2013, I found out I was accepted. I was stunned at how much credit Georgetown was willing to award me from my time in the military. I'd submitted a transcript from the Department of Defense, which listed every training course I did in the marines, every class I completed, every correspondence course I took. The correspondence courses were like ongoing education classes you could take to help get promoted. There were a ton of them in all different subject areas, like land navigation, math for marines, desert ops, history of the Marine Corps, and so on. You register, and the corps sends you a textbook and a Scantron test. You read the book, take the test, then send it back. During my first enlistment, I took a bunch of them because I was so bored. I was expecting Georgetown to write off most of that work. For many schools, veterans are guaranteed paychecks; the G.I. Bill is government money, and they want to cash in by making us take unnecessary courses. But the school gave me sixty-two credits—enough that I could get my degree in less than three years if I wanted to. I really respected and appreciated that.

That fall, I started as a probationary student. If I earned a high-enough GPA my first semester, I'd be permitted to enroll full-time. Starting out part-time was a perfect way for me to test the water.

I started out taking a writing class and a poli-sci class (the one where Josh and I met). Within the first week, I knew I was in the right place. In the writing class, the professor was tough, and a lot of the students hated her assignments, but I loved them. I'd benefited from the time I'd had away from school. I was ready to dive back in, doing close reads of texts like *To Kill a Mockingbird* and *All Quiet on the Western Front*. I wrote an essay every week. At my job, I felt that I could do my work in my sleep, but at school it felt like I was really chewing on something substantial.

I did well in both classes and decided to leave my job at the DIA and enroll full-time. It was an easy decision. The only thing I liked about my job was the people I worked with. We had become close, and I knew that when I left, that wouldn't change. Plus, working and going to school at the same time was tough, and I didn't want to half-ass it. Now that I knew I could do the work, I wanted to devote all my energy to my degree. As an adult, going to school felt different. I was excited about going to class, reading the books, writing the essays, and completing assignments.

Along with my academic schedule, I had tried out for and made the club hockey team at Georgetown. I hadn't played competitive hockey in more than ten years, but I'd started playing on a team of veterans the year before and I was still in good shape. I wasn't sure I'd get along with the kids on the college team; I assumed that they'd all be bratty prep-school types. I was wrong. They were hockey players. They accepted me with open arms, and before I knew it I was the starting left winger. We dominated the league, winning the championship that year. The team held the record for most titles in league history, and I was proud to be a part of the program. Playing competitive hockey with a great group of guys added to my renewed sense of purpose. I loved lining up for face-offs and looking at the kid on the other team right in the face. I was older than my opponents by ten years and I had twenty pounds on most of them. With my long beard and "old man strength," I quickly developed a reputation in the league as a heavy-hitting power forward. I was alive again.

It was also a good feeling to meet new people through school, especially fellow vets like Josh. In joking about his prosthetic that first day of class, we became instant buddies. Every so often we hung out outside of class at a bar or Capitals game. Josh didn't live too far from me, so occasionally we'd grab a few drinks at my favorite pub in the neighborhood, the Pug. A classic dive, the place felt more like somebody's basement than a bar. It was small and narrow, with a long wooden bar on one side and walls covered in old framed photos and sports team banners.

After we were good and warm from a few rounds of drinks one night, Josh and I swapped our stories from *over there,* the way that beer and veteran camaraderie made it easier to do. Josh had been an infantryman in the army for about four years when he deployed to Zabul Province in southern Afghanistan, just northeast of Helmand, where I'd been. He described the beginning of his deployment as pretty routine. He was in a mounted vehicle unit, which meant the team could travel a lot farther than traditional infantry companies did on foot. The vehicles—called Strykers—looked like tanks, but with huge wheels instead of treads. Each one typically carried eleven guys. On their initial patrols, they engaged in some sporadic pockets of fighting with the Taliban, but it was "nothing like the movies," Josh said.

Josh had only been in-country a little over three months when his vehicle hit the roadside bomb that took his leg. It was a routine patrol on a clear day, middle of the week, September 2009. Josh was in the first vehicle in the convoy, on the machine gun, sitting in a way that was against protocol: kind of half in and half out of the vehicle. When the Stryker hit the pressure plate, the IED exploded directly under them. Not only did the blast take Josh's right leg, but it took the lives of three of Josh's teammates inside. The fact that Josh had been sitting the way he had was what saved his life.

In the first few weeks after the accident, Josh had a bunch of surgeries; remarkably, within a few months, he was up and walking. Motivated by his initial success, he made steady progress for a couple of years, but all the follow-up surgeries he required between 2011 and 2015 started making it really hard for him to get on with life. How could he keep a job if as soon as he got one, he'd have to turn around and request a couple of months off for surgery and recovery?

When we talked, Josh had a way of keeping positive. Understandably, he was more comfortable talking about what came after the accident than the accident itself. He would say things like how much he benefited from top-tier health care and how lucky he was to have been injured at a time when advancements in prosthetics allowed him to regain so much independence. He always was happy to show me—and anyone who asked—his leg and how it worked. Josh was grateful to be alive, and he wanted to move forward.

For two guys, a dog, and a twenty-seven-year-old truck with no air-conditioning, driving from the Grand Canyon to Los Angeles—about eight hours through the Mojave Desert—is a pilgrimage. As we made our way through the 100-something-degree heat, across the flat, arid terrain, my eyes steadily flickered between the road and the temperature gauge. I didn't say it aloud to Josh, but I thought for sure the engine would overheat. *C'mon, baby,* I thought to myself, watching the needle hover between the c and h marks. So far, our faithful Land Cruiser was doing okay.

Every so often, a current of wind brought a gust of sand right through the car. A fine layer of it began coating the dashboard, our skin, and everything in between, even working its way between our teeth. Naturally, we were smiling from ear to ear. Even though I was nervous about the engine, I never once envied the people in their SUVs who blew by us with frost on their windows.

"Fred probably thinks we're taking him back to Afghanistan," Josh joked. I laughed and looked up in the rearview mirror, but Fred was asleep, unbothered by the desert air whipping through his white fur.

Ahead of us, the heat made the horizon waver, as if layers of road were continually peeling off and evaporating into the sky. I kept my foot steady on the gas, and we pressed on, giving the Land Cruiser encouragement by patting the dash.

As we finally breached the end of the great Mojave, we pulled into a small service station to celebrate. The Land Cruiser needed gas, and the three of us needed water and ice cream. I filled the tank, then pulled the truck into the shade and popped the hood. Josh, Fred, and I sat at a picnic table near the pumps and, under a faded plastic umbrella, enjoyed our soft-serve ice cream in sugar cones. After eating half my cone, I gave the rest to Fred. Specks of sand from my beard had settled into the melting ice cream, but Fred didn't seem to notice the grit as he scarfed down the treat.

Back on the road, continuing farther west, signs of civilization began to interrupt the barren landscape: billboards, faded strip malls, parking lots. Then, as we crept closer to L.A., we encountered another phenomenon of civilization: the traffic jam. We came to a crawl on the freeway and looked out at our fellow travelers—commuters in BMWs and Land Rovers, in big sunglasses, with phones in their hands. The Land Cruiser might as well have been a covered wagon, and inside it, we must have looked like quite the sight: two dusty, bearded, sweaty guys in tank tops accompanied by one panting, short-legged dog hanging out the window in the middle of rush hour.

We inched our way to our exit. The plan was to stay the night with Josh's friend Kyle. Josh and Kyle had deployed together but hadn't seen one another since Afghanistan. After Josh's vehicle hit the IED and he was taken from the battlefield, Kyle's deployment ended in a similarly horrific fashion. Kyle had been a sniper, and during a gunfight with the Taliban, a single round hit him in three locations. As he held his rifle and looked down the scope, a Taliban bullet grazed his left wrist, traveled through his right thumb, then ricocheted off the buttstock of his gun into his right shoulder. The wounds were serious, but he survived.

Kyle met us outside his apartment building, wearing a tank top, cutoff camo shorts, and flip-flops. His blond hair fell nearly to his shoulders, though some of it was stuffed in a bun on top of his head. You couldn't see that he'd been injured. He looked as if he'd come from a day of surfing or from a music festival.

With a big smile on his face, Kyle gave Josh a big hug and a pat on the back, sending dust from the Mojave into the air. The three of us—all veterans of desert warfare—couldn't help but laugh. Turning to me with the same big grin, Kyle said, "You must be Craig—and *this* must be Fred! I've heard a lot about this little guy. Welcome to L.A., Freddy!" He bent down to pet Fred and I smiled at Kyle's drawn-out way of speaking: a classic Southern California accent.

Even though Kyle's unit was on the fourth floor, the low ceilings made the place feel dark. Dust hung in the air where strips of light came through. There were dirty dishes in the sink and on the counters, shoes and magazines strewn about the living room. On the walls were Jimi Hendrix and Bob Dylan posters, as well as an American flag. Kyle pointed to a plaque that displayed the stock of his sniper rifle. You could see the scar in its side from the bullet. It commemorated his brush with death, Kyle said.

The apartment kind of reminded me of a college dorm room—it made you want to throw open the shades and let the air and light in. Fred jumped onto the couch and made himself at home while Josh and I took turns showering off the desert dirt. When I came out, Kyle had put on the nineties action flick *Point Break.*

"Ha! I love this movie," I said, sitting down next to him. It had been in regular rotation for movie night back on Leatherneck.

Kyle laughed and finished rolling a joint on the coffee table. "Helps me with the pain from my surgeries," he said, bringing the joint to his lips and sparking his lighter.

"You don't have to explain, man. I'm sure it's better than whatever the VA was trying to get you to take," I said.

Physically, Kyle looked completely fine. If he had scarring from his injury, it wasn't immediately obvious. I wondered if going through a trauma like that, then looking totally "normal" afterward, made it tough for him.

"Meds made the pain go away but made a lot of other things come around," Kyle said, then paused to suck in another hit. "Felt like my brain was betraying me."

I nodded and leaned back into the couch, eyes on the TV.

That night, Josh and I saw a side of L.A. we probably never would have if we hadn't met up with Kyle. The evening turned into a sort of bar crawl through strange, kitschy dive bars, including a memorable one that was hosting death metal karaoke. A skinny kid in even skinnier jeans took the stage all by himself and put on a hell of a show, screaming along to some obscure heavy metal song. It was too weird not to love.

The next day, we said our good-byes to Kyle and thanked him for putting us up for the night. He offered to let us stay longer, but we were ready to be on our way. My buddy Casey had offered to put us up for a few days at his place in Venice, and we were eager to explore another part of the city.

Driving away from Kyle's apartment, Josh let out a sigh. I could tell he felt uncomfortable about his friend and the state of his place.

"It's fine, man," I said, but I understood how he felt. Josh knew Kyle as a sniper in the army, back when Kyle performed one of the most physically and emotionally demanding jobs in the world. Now, you just got the impression that he might not be doing so well.

"I'm not sure what to think," Josh said.

"Yeah, it's tricky, man," I said. "I mean, it looked like he was paying the bills. He's in school. He's probably happy, you know?" Josh hadn't known Kyle before the army; maybe this was how he'd always been.

As vets, we didn't exactly spend our time sitting around talking about post-traumatic stress, asking personal questions, exchanging notes. The stigma is so intense that you don't want to heap it on anybody. Plus, everybody's experience is different; PTS looks different for different people. Some vets have very painful, debilitating post-traumatic stress. For others, it's not like that. And for others, maybe it's not there at all. Assuming anything is a mistake; it only feeds into the stereotype that all combat vets are "broken."

Venice Beach was a circus. Walking down the beachside promenade, Josh, my buddy Casey, and I took in the sights around us: masked unicyclists, tattooed jugglers, hulking body-builders, impassioned musicians, face-painted performers. When we stopped to watch a juggler, Fred looked up inquisitively, following each ball as it traveled up, down, up, down, waiting for one to drop. We watched him watching the balls and laughed. It was a beautiful sunny day. Palm trees rose up overhead, the mountains looked down on us in the distance, and the Pacific Ocean sparkled. So this is what all those California songs are about, I thought.

Casey and I first met during intelligence training in Virginia Beach. After training, we'd crossed paths briefly at Leatherneck, but hadn't seen each other since then. He was one of those guys who was a friend for life, though. It was easy to pick back up.

Off the boardwalk, we found a skate park where kids were competing. A DJ played hip-hop while an announcer called out names of skaters when it was their turn. We stood and watched the young skaters push the limits of gravity and physics. Fred sat quietly and followed the skaters with his head. Back home in D.C., he usually tried to chase skateboarders, howling and pulling on his leash. But here, he seemed to be enjoying the entertainment. One of the skaters took a spill just in front of us, and Fred let out a high-pitched yowl, going *OOOH!* as if to say, "*Ouch!*" His reaction drew some laughs from the otherwise tough-looking crowd.

We spent the week at Casey's place, enjoying having some downtime in the air-conditioning. In the mornings, I'd take Fred for a walk, then we'd go up to the rooftop deck together to enjoy the cool morning breeze coming off the ocean while I drank a fresh mug of coffee. From Casey's, I also got in touch with someone I hadn't seen since Afghanistan: Top. He lived in Oceanside, just a couple of hours south, and invited us to come down. Top hadn't seen Fred since the day he helped me smuggle the dog onto the helicopter in Afghanistan. I couldn't wait to reunite them.

Top lived just outside of Camp Pendleton, the base I'd been stationed at right before and after my deployment. Pulling into the neighborhood, we drove by big suburban houses with USMC flags on front porches and eagle, globe, and anchor stickers in car windows. Top's house was no exception. He had a black pickup truck parked out front, and I smiled when I saw a red Harley-Davidson sitting next to it.

Top walked through the open garage door. He looked the same—broad shoulders, huge frame, slicked-back hair, huge smile. He wore a Harley T-shirt, shorts, and flip-flops.

"Hey, boys!" he bellowed. "Where's that stubby-legged guy that used to leave his chewed-up rope on my sleeping bag?"

Fred, who had just jumped down from the Land Cruiser and was on the end of his leash, pulled frantically. I let go and he

ran right up to Top, howling the whole way with joy. His body
waved from snout to butt as he wagged his tail.

Top squatted down and Fred ran right into his arms, gleefully shivering and spinning and wiggling, till Top scooped him
up and cradled him like a baby. The dog licked his face and
nuzzled his salt-and-pepper hair.

I don't think any of us expected Fred to react the way he did.
It'd been five long years, and the last time he'd seen Top was
half a world away. Still, it didn't matter. To Fred, it was as if no
time had passed. He never even liked for people to pick him up,
but with Top, he didn't mind at all.

Top hoisted Fred in the crook of his left arm, then walked
over to Josh and me. He shook Josh's hand and introduced himself, then pulled me in for a bear hug.

"Good to see you, brother," he said before releasing me.
"Thank you for coming."

"And it's really good to see you, you little weirdo," he said,
looking Fred in the face. They were both smiling so widely that
their eyes disappeared.

Top led us through the garage into the house, explaining that
he had his smoker going out back with some salmon and pork
shoulder for us. Walking through the garage, I noticed a squat
rack, kegorator, and an iconic marine black flag with a skull,
crossed rifles, and yellow letters that read, MESS WITH THE BEST,
DIE LIKE THE REST.

Inside, we were greeted by Top's wife, Tara, who embraced
and welcomed us. "We're so glad you're here," she said. "This
guy's been pacing around all day waiting for you to arrive," she
added, smiling at Top.

"I know who he's really excited about seeing," I said, laughing. Fred hadn't left Top's side. Tara knelt down and gave Fred a big kiss on his head. "Thanks for looking after my man while he was in your country. I'm so glad you made it back safe and sound."

From the glass door leading to the backyard, Top's own dogs excitedly peered inside at us, pressing their snouts to the glass to try and get a look. There were three of them—two big shepherd mixes and one smaller one. Clearly it was no mistake Fred and Top had gravitated toward each other back in Sangin. Top was a dog person.

Tecates in hand, we went out back and let the dogs introduce themselves as only dogs can. After a minute or so, they seemed to reach an understanding. Fred instantly picked out Top's biggest dog, Sugar Bear, as his new best buddy. They began chasing each other, spinning around and trying to nip each other's legs.

With the dogs romping around, I turned to Top and said something about admiring his smoker and looking forward to dinner. He looked me in the eye and said, "It's Mark. I don't go by Top anymore." I could tell by his voice that he was firm, like he'd given it some serious thought. Every rank in the Marine Corps has a nickname, and the master sergeant is Top, so, over there, that's all we ever called him. Some retired guys still like to be called by their rank after getting out—maybe it's just what they're used to or they don't want to let go or it just reminds them of the good old days. Top had spent over twenty years in the RECON community—a rare and remarkable achievement, which also meant he'd seen his share of "good old days" as well as all the dark that comes with them. If he wanted to be called Mark, I'm sure he had his reasons.

We all sat around out back, Mark occasionally checking on the meat, all of us nursing our beers. It was another perfect Southern California day: mild with a bright blue sky overhead. The dogs continued to chase one another. Fred got confused by the doggy door leading into the house. He'd never used one before, but after watching Mark's dogs a few times, he bravely made the leap. With his short legs and long body, he wasn't exactly designed for a contraption like that, but after he made it through once, he kept going in and out, mastering his new trick.

When he got tired, Fred came over and sat on Mark's foot, turning his head back to look up at him. I pictured Top and Fred alone in the command center in Sangin, a little clay room with a huge black antenna sticking out. Each night when we went out on patrols, that's where they sat. The room was cramped and windowless, and colossal bags of rice lined the walls. Someone had created a makeshift desk out of a plank of wood, where Top sat. The only light came from the glow of the Toughbook laptop—where Top monitored a map of the night's route—and the green flicker of the lights from the CB radios. At designated check-in points, the lieutenant would radio Top: *"Checkpoint Alpha"* or *"Checkpoint Bravo,"* they'd say, *"Nothing new to report."* *"Roger that,"* Top would respond. It went on all night. I never saw Top sleep. If we lost contact on a patrol, he'd know where to send the QRF. If we stepped on an IED, he'd know where to send the medevac. And as Top would work through the night—a big guy hunched over a tiny table, staring into a screen—a little dog would sit on his boot.

Mark leaned down and petted Fred around his ears.

"I remember one time over there, I caught this little guy stealing jerky from my ruck. He sniffed it out somehow. He had his whole face buried into my bag up to his eyeballs before I caught him," Mark remembered, smiling. "I was too impressed to be mad at him. Gave him half the bag."

"Well, you were pretty much his personal chef," I said, remembering how I'd started catching Top slipping Fred little bites of food around the compound. Sometimes, after we got a drop-off of fresh MREs, all the guys and I would eagerly tear open a bunch of meals but wouldn't finish them all. Top hated when we did it; it was wasteful. So he'd gather up the leftover food and make little concoctions out of them for Fred. Once he took half a meatloaf patty and mashed it up with pasta shells in white sauce. Fred, of course, loved it.

One by one, Mark's three daughters came home from school or from their activities. They were all about high school age, with the oldest getting ready to go off to college. Like Tara, they were polite and well spoken, pulling up chairs outside and sitting to talk with all of us. When the whole family was home and Mark deemed the meat ready, we went inside and all sat around the dining room table for a proper dinner. I couldn't remember the last time I'd sat down like that for a family meal. I was grateful, and the food was delicious.

Over dinner that night, I told the girls what an honor it was to work alongside their dad in Afghanistan. He was the kind of leader that didn't need to yell or scream to get people to follow him. You followed him because you wanted to be like him, you wanted to be around him, and you didn't want to let him down.

And I wanted to thank him, earnestly, for keeping us safe over there. It was his leadership and the decisions he made for the company—patrolling only at night, taking challenging off-road routes, never using the same route twice—that kept us out of harm's way.

"We were really lucky," Mark said, downplaying any credit I tried to give him. After our deployment together, Mark had retired. I could only imagine the impact he'd made on the lives of so many other marines like me.

Driving back to L.A. that night, in the quiet of the car, I thought back to Kyle in his smoky, dark apartment. From our short time with him and then with Mark, it was easy to get the impression that maybe Mark's life post-Afghanistan was going more smoothly than Kyle's. But I also knew we'd only gotten a glimpse, and there was really no sure way to tell how either of our buddies were processing their own combat experiences. For Mark, did having a family and a big house help, or could it make it even harder to readjust? Did Kyle's relaxed lifestyle, with fewer responsibilities, help him ease back to post-army life, or did he feel isolated?

I didn't know the answers. Everyone's reaction to combat is different. For me, I struggled to feel anything when I came home. The bar for what excited and moved me had been set impossibly high from my time in Sangin. I had seen death up close, and it gave me a sense of how fragile life was while also making me somewhat indifferent to people's feelings. "It could be worse" became a common phrase of mine. I didn't elaborate on my feelings because I didn't realize I was having any. I carried on with my life, went to my ten-year high school reunion, and reconnected with my friends from home. Inside, a part of me was screaming out for help, but I didn't listen. I had too much to be thankful for to be messed up. I had come home, and I had all my body parts, a great dog, and a fun group of friends.

The attitude we had in the field was that anything could be fixed with Motrin and water. Like the marines around me, I had a lot of pride. Once I got home, I didn't want to be told I was "sick" with something like post-traumatic stress. I didn't want to feel like a victim or be treated like one. I knew PTS had nothing to do with being strong or weak or with having enough willpower or not, but it still took me a while to listen to that voice inside me and find my way.

CHAPTER 10

Leatherneck

When the helicopter touched down at Leatherneck, we took turns helping each other up, and I lifted Fred in the duffel bag, carefully tucking him under my arm. It was strange to be able to walk down the ramp, not run. The flat asphalt of the tarmac was so solid and smooth that for a moment I felt dizzy, like I was stepping on land for the first time after a month at sea. The sun was bright overhead, and as we walked across the flight line, the wind from the rotors shook loose a cloud of dust from our uniforms.

There was a big welcome reception for us right there on the airfield, complete with pizza and cold Gatorade. I hadn't had a cold drink in weeks, but I was going to have to wait a little longer. With my four-legged contraband tucked under my arm, I broke off from the guys and ducked between a row of HESCO barriers—huge, dirt-filled barrels—that lined the flight line, making my way toward the road I hoped Sergio would drive in on.

Behind the barriers, I took a knee and looked anxiously into the distance. Fred shook and squirmed in the bag. I opened the zipper and let him pop his head out. He sniffed the air and scanned around, panting and blinking under the hot sun.

When I first arrived on base, months earlier, the sheer size of Leatherneck had shocked me. There were three different chow halls at least, a hospital, clinics, a post office, and rows and rows of office buildings, tents, and barracks. Big enough to drive around and get lost. There were four state-of-the-art gyms, too—that was important. Marines don't mind sleeping in the dirt, but they want a nice gym. There was a huge Internet lounge where you could get a cup of coffee and play video games like Call of Duty—you know, in case you needed a little more "modern warfare" in your life. Camp Bastion, the British-run base with an airfield, was connected to Leatherneck, too. That's where all the helicopters, Osprey, and drones came in and out of. The whole place was so extensive, you could almost forget you were in Afghanistan altogether.

At Leatherneck, you felt pretty safe. You could move freely. You'd see civilian contractors walking from building to building and marines driving around in civilian vehicles. You were supposed to carry your rifle with you at all times, unloaded, with one magazine of ammo in your pocket, just in case. The way guys carried them, though, you'd think they were yoga mats instead of weapons. Some even taped over their magazine wells to keep dust out because they didn't want the hassle of cleaning them.

A lot of marines spent their entire deployment on Leatherneck. If you worked in supply or if you were an intel analyst, like many of the guys I worked with, Leatherneck was probably the only piece of Afghanistan you were ever going to see. Every job was important, but I was grateful to have spent as much time in the field as I did.

Finally, from behind the HESCO barriers, I caught sight of a little black Toyota pickup bopping down the dirt road, kicking up a dusty cloud in its wake. It had to be Sergio and Mac. As the Toyota came nearer, I spotted Sergio behind the wheel and McGuire with his oversize cowboy grin beside him. They started to pull up next to my hiding spot, and before they pulled to a full stop, I grabbed Fred and threw him and myself over the side of the truck bed.

The diesel engine let out a groan as Sergio shifted gears and we lurched forward, speeding away from the flight line toward our barracks on the opposite side of the base. I unzipped the duffel bag all the way, letting Fred venture out. He struggled to keep his balance as we bounced down the road. I chuckled to myself as I realized that he'd flown on a helicopter before riding in a car.

"You look like hell, man!" Sergio shouted from the cab, grinning and handing me a bottle of water. I took a swig and was shocked by how strange it felt to drink something cold. I found a plastic cup rolling around in the back of the truck and poured some for Fred.

Leatherneck was always expanding and changing. When I'd gotten back from Trek Nawa, I noticed a Pizza Hut had opened up while I'd been away. The whole place seemed to grow by the day. This time, as we drove toward the barracks, I spotted a compound off to the side of the road that hadn't been there when I left. In bright red letters against a yellow background, a small sign near its entrance read: DHL.

Sergio pulled up to our barracks. The long white trailers were lined with bunks and slept about ten guys each. Ours was pretty empty at the time, which worked in my and Fred's favor. Plus, I knew I could trust my teammates.

I plopped Fred down on my bunk.

"Hey, Freddy, here's your first bed," I said. Impressed, the dusty dog curled up right there, blinking his eyes sleepily and letting out a sigh.

Sergio, Mac, and I stood around looking at him. The guys laughed, and so did I. Here we were with a dog in our barracks. After talking for a few minutes, Mac said, "Hey, man, go get a shower. We'll stay with the little guy." It was his polite way of telling me I smelled like hot garbage.

The water felt amazing. I turned it as hot as it would go and stood under the faucet, letting the pressure rinse the sand from my hair. Brown water pooled at my feet. Afterward, I scraped away my beard and put on fresh cammies. The starchy pants were so clean they felt stiff, the weight of them foreign against my thighs.

We spent the rest of the afternoon camped out in the barracks with Fred. Mac brought us some food from the chow hall, and we watched a few movies on my laptop. I found some rope and planned to use it as a leash for Fred. Once it was good and dark, Mac kept a lookout while I escorted the dog outside.

"My dog back home would've peed in my boots by now!" Mac joked as he opened the door for us.

The night was clear and cool. Our barracks were at the end of the row, so we didn't have to go far before we could duck behind some HESCO barriers and walk into a field where we were relatively covered. Not many people drove around at night. Fred was calm; he didn't struggle against the leash or make a sound. In the dark, his white fur seemed to almost glow against the moon-dusted earth. I watched as he sniffed around, nose to the ground, finding places to mark. Once he was done, we went straight back inside. Sometimes, with Fred, I had this feeling that he knew what was going on. He had a way of cooperating.

That night, lying in bed with the dog between my knees, I was too anxious to sleep. I would be going back to Sangin after a two-week break on base. The clock was already ticking for Fred. I needed to get him out before going back into the field. The image of the DHL compound I'd spotted on our drive came back to me. The shipping company had likely popped up to fulfill the growing commercial shipping demands on Leatherneck. We already had a post office, staffed by military members, but they mostly handled troop mail and care packages. DHL, though, was its own company. Instead of military staff, they'd have their own civilian workers, just like plenty of other facilities on base, from the chow halls to construction projects. Getting civilians to help me seemed safer than involving other marines. The place was crawling with military police, but the civilian-run contractor buildings were sort of off the radar. If Fred was going to get shipped home, DHL would be his ticket out.

The next morning, with Fred stowed away in the barracks, I pulled up outside the DHL compound. The whole area was surrounded by a twelve-foot chain-link fence, concealed with green mesh. I walked up to the gate, which was closed but not locked. I pushed it open just enough to squeeze through.

The place looked as if it had been abandoned. There was no one around. A forklift was parked just inside the gate, unoccupied. In the back, a few trailers sat quietly in a row—probably sleeping quarters. Propped up against one of them, I spotted a small yellow sign that read OFFICE in red letters. With low expectations, I made my way over.

I tapped on the door, and it swung open. Directly inside was a cheap, wobbly-looking desk with a computer monitor and keyboard. From underneath it, I heard a man with what I thought was a thick Ugandan accent. "Come in!" he said as he lifted his hand above his head and waved it in the air.

The DHL worker picked himself up off the floor with a groan and wiped his forehead with a white towel. Without looking at me, he pressed his index finger against the power button—tapping incessantly—until the computer whirred to life. A satisfied smile on his face, he finally turned to me.

"Yes, Sergeant. What can I do for you?" he said.

"Please, call me Craig," I told him.

The man smiled and nodded his head as he came around the desk with his hand outstretched.

"Okay, Craig. My name is Tinashe. It is nice to meet you. And what can I do for you?"

Tinashe was about five foot eight, and I'd guess in his forties. He had a bald head, bare face, and dark skin. With his blue DHL polo shirt tucked into his belted khakis, he looked sharp, and he smiled generously.

"I'm thinking of shipping something, but it looks like you guys aren't quite up and running yet," I said, scanning the room.

Tinashe smiled even bigger and said, "Oh, don't worry, my friend! We'll be up and running within twenty-four hours.

Things move quickly here, I make sure of that. What were you thinking of shipping?"

I took a quick breath and tried to sound smooth. "If someone had a dog—hypothetically—would that be something you could ship?"

Tinashe looked at me, not letting the smile drop from his face. "How big is this dog?" he asked, crossing his arms across his chest.

"Oh, I'm just curious if—" I started to say, but Tinashe, starting to laugh, cut me off.

"Bring him over! I want to meet this dog!" he said.

"Okay, man," I said, giving in. "I'll bring him over here tomorrow."

"I can't make any promises, but I will promise you I'll do what I can," he said.

First thing the following morning, I snuck Fred into the pickup, making him ride on the floor of the passenger side. We drove toward DHL, cautiously passing by a military police SUV parked outside the chow hall.

When we pulled into the gate of the compound, I was shocked to see it had completely transformed. It was as if everything had come to life. The forklift operator lifted a pallet of water bottles onto a flatbed truck. Tinashe stood, wearing the same blue polo, clipboard in hand, giving orders to workers as they zipped around. When he saw me, he waved me over to a parking spot by the office.

Fred had popped up onto the passenger seat now, and when Tinashe got a look at him, his face lit up. He went over to Fred's side and opened the door for him.

"Look at this funny guy! You didn't tell me he was such a

good-looking dog!" Tinashe said as Fred spilled out onto the dusty ground, excitedly prancing around Tinashe's feet.

We walked into the same office from the day before, and Tinashe handed me a printout.

"That is a list of forms that you'll need to get this guy home," he said, bending to rub Fred behind the ears. "What is his name, by the way?"

"Oh, I'm sorry—this is Fred," I told him.

Tinashe erupted in laughter.

"Fred!" he roared. "Fred the Afghan with the American friend!"

I couldn't help but laugh, too. A couple of the DHL workers wandered in to see what all the commotion was about. One of them introduced himself as Peter, and we got talking. Peter was from the Philippines, here in Afghanistan to make some cash and send it home to his family. He said most of his coworkers were Filipino, too. Well-paying jobs in the Philippines were hard to come by, and Peter had traveled half a world away to support his loved ones. Most of the bases I'd been on were staffed by third-country nationals (TCNs) like Tinashe and Peter. They were people from one country—like the Philippines—working in another country—like Afghanistan—for a company from a third country—like the U.S.-run DHL. During my time at Gitmo, most of the TCNs on base were Jamaican. I made friends with a few guys who drove the buses. Before I left, we swapped T-shirts: I gave them my unit T-shirts and they gave me work shirts. I had immense respect for the sacrifices they were making to survive and support their families back home.

Tinashe pointed to a huge chart on the wall. It was a long list of things they weren't permitted to ship—mostly obvious stuff like grenades, rifles, bullets, spent cartridges.

"There's nothing here about live animals, my friend," he said to me with a wide grin.

I was grateful to Tinashe, overwhelmed by his willingness to be so helpful. Excitedly, I thanked him, and Fred and I made our way back to the barracks.

Back in the room, my heart sank. Tinashe's list was long, including forms that sounded near impossible to obtain—like serialized customs forms and multiple veterinary certifications, one of which required proof of a rabies vaccination and a thirty-day quarantine supervised by a veterinarian. How the hell was I going to get that?

I pulled out my satellite phone and called Sarah, but she didn't pick up. Rambling nervously, I left a long voice mail describing each of the forms I needed, asking her to find out if she could get her hands on them and mail them to me.

I looked at Fred, sitting on the bed. He looked back at me with raised eyebrows as if asking, "What now?"

Over the next few days, I corresponded with Sarah, who was making all the phone calls she could back home, trying to find someone who knew anything about getting a live animal shipped from Afghanistan to the U.S. Meanwhile, hiding Fred in the barracks was becoming increasingly stressful. There were rumors going around that rooms were being inspected. First sergeants were coming by looking for booze and other contraband, making sure our rooms were clean and beds were made. Under normal circumstances it would have pissed me off—we weren't in boot camp anymore—but with Fred in our room, I was terrified. There were no locks on the door; anyone could come in at any time.

After a few days of hiding Fred, I thought, *I can't do this anymore, I'm going to get caught.* I went over to the EOD compound and talked to Matt and Dave, who had told me they'd help hide him. Their compound was farther from most of the activity on Leatherneck, and their command was a little more lax. We all agreed it would be easier for Fred to be stowed away with them, and I drove him over that night.

The next time I talked to Sarah, though, it was becoming clearer that shipping Fred back to the States was going to be more time consuming than I imagined. She hadn't had any luck with the forms yet, and once she did, it was going to take time to mail them. The days were slipping by. I realized I had to shift my focus from sending Fred home to finding a way to keep him safe while I went out on my next mission. I hated the thought of leaving him on Leatherneck without me, but I didn't have any other choice.

The safest place on Leatherneck would be with civilians. If Sergio or Mac had to hide Fred in the barracks for weeks, it would only be a matter of time till someone caught them. Same with the EOD guys. Plus, Dave and Matt were both finished with their deployment. They were going home. The more I considered the options, the more it became clear: I had to ask Tinashe if he could hide Fred at the DHL compound.

Around dusk one day, I put Fred in the truck and we drove to DHL. The setting sun and desert haze turned the sky yellow in its last breaths of daylight. When we pulled up to the compound, Fred and I hopped out and met Tinashe in the office.

The words came tumbling out.

"Tinashe, I've got a problem. I'm going back out in another week. I'll be gone for a while—like a month—and I don't know what I'm going to do with Fred. We've been trying to hide him, but if we get caught, he'll be put down," I said. "My sister is working on the customs forms, but she needs more time . . ."

Tinashe stood from petting Fred and placed his hand on my shoulder.

"My friend, didn't I tell you I would do what I could? Fred will stay here with me while you are gone. This is a special dog, and I want to do my part to make sure he gets to America."

The way he said it, it was like I didn't even have to explain. I leaned in and hugged him. Tinashe walked outside and, moving like a hummingbird, quickly put together a plan. He picked up a long ratchet strap. "Here," he said, tying it to a metal pole. "While we're working all day, Fred can stay here."

Peter and a few of the guys appeared. It was the end of the workday, and they were off the clock. Behind the office, in front of the line of trailers, a folding table hosted a few simmering Crock-Pots. It was dinnertime, and hearing the news about Fred, they brought over a plate of chicken and rice for him.

Each of us was from a different country—continent, even— yet here we all were, brought together by this one little mutt in the middle of the Afghanistan desert. We were all transplants here, trying to survive in our strange circumstances. These guys didn't have to help me, and still, they did. I was humbled by their generosity.

As I slipped away, back to the truck, and drove away from the compound, Fred barely noticed. He knew he was going to be well taken care of there, and he was happy.

Two weeks at Leatherneck had hardly felt like one. Aside from getting Fred situated, I had to prep for the next mission, spending hours upon hours in the intel office with Sergio while he briefed me on what to expect from the Taliban this time out.

The plan was to reinsert a few miles north of where we'd been before, continuing to clear out the Taliban along Highway 611. Our aim was to establish a patrol base that would serve as a semi-permanent fixture along the highway and secure the area so the engineers could continue to make their way toward the dam.

The farther north we went, the narrower the Green Zone became, cut off by an eastward bend in the Helmand River. It was kind of like a bottleneck—a narrow swath of Green Zone dense with Taliban. From our experience in Sangin, along with coverage from drones we used to track movement, we could tell that the Taliban had been "commuting" down from this area in the north to attack us during the day, then retreating back at night. After we extracted, we monitored the area by drone and saw the Taliban move around completely at ease, balls out, unafraid. They raided villagers' homes and patrolled the area with AK-47s. It was almost as if we'd never been there. It was troubling. This time, we were going to show up right in their kitchen.

On my first missions, since I was the only member of the company with my specific job—an attachment human-intelligence collector—I'd ended up getting closest with other attachments, like Ali, our interpreter, who actually had a contract position, and Matt and Dave, the EOD guys. Ali was going out on this next mission again, but Dave and Matt had already been in Afghanistan for eight months and were heading home.

Another EOD team had just arrived in-country to replace them: Justin and Ysa.

We met the night of our reinsertion. A bunch of us were gathering on the flight line with our gear, cracking jokes and killing time. I told a story about how I'd smoked a cigar with one of the British marines in Sangin, then promptly got sick just as we stepped off on a patrol. I spent the night meeting villagers with a puke-stained uniform.

The guys all laughed, and when Justin and Ysa joined us, I turned to introduce myself.

"Hey, guys. I'm Craig," I said. I liked to skip titles and marine formalities to throw people off guard and gauge their reaction.

Justin was about my height, a big guy, in shape, with these huge hands. I could tell immediately he had a quiet confidence. I knew he was a staff sergeant, but he introduced himself as I had, using just his first name. After shaking hands, he seemed to take my casual tone as an opening to ask about Fred.

"You're the guy who snuck the dog out in a duffel bag last time out, right?" Justin said.

Dave must have blabbed about Operation Fred. Justin was a new guy—I couldn't let him off that easy, so I changed the subject.

"Dude, you're from Pittsburgh, aren't you? I'd recognize that accent anywhere, you freaking yinzer."

Justin immediately cracked a smile. I told him my dad's side of the family was from a small town outside of Pittsburgh. Everytime my dad said "house," it sounded like "hass." I hadn't heard the western-Pennsylvanian accent in a while but I still had an ear for it.

To make it even, I busted on Ysa about his name. "Y-S-A?" I said, pronouncing it *why-essay* in a goofy tone. Ysa—which is actually pronounced *ee-ssa*—was, like Justin, immediately easygoing. He was a little shorter than Justin, a Mexican American guy from a small town in Texas, but his personality was as big as the state itself.

"Look, guys. Me and Dave were close," I said. "The RECON guys are great, but they're their own unit. We should stick together." Justin and Ysa had more combat experience than I did, but this would be their first time in Sangin.

"Okay—let's be friends," Ysa said with a smile, and they lugged their gear over so we could load up on the helicopter together.

As the sun sank into the dusty horizon, I felt a moment of peace. Fred was safe. I knew Sarah would find a way to get the forms we needed. And I was surrounded by a good team of guys, doing a job I loved. I didn't know it then, but that moment was the quiet before the storm. As the light faded in the sky, we trekked across the tarmac, boarded the helicopters, and headed back to Sangin.

CHAPTER 11

Wilderness

On our last night in Los Angeles, Jen, a friend of mine from high school, and her husband, Barry, hosted a small party at their home in Echo Park. The last time I'd seen Jen was about fifteen years before, at her high school graduation party. Since then, she'd kept up with me on social media and told me she was dying to meet Fred. When we got to their place, it felt like no time had passed at all.

That night, Jen and Barry were amazing hosts. Barry grilled swordfish, octopus, and veggies out on the patio and served up homemade salsa while Jen floated between guests, introducing us to friends and making all of us feel at home.

At one point, when Jen and I were standing in the kitchen, she surprised me by remembering the speech I'd given to our class at the end of our senior year.

"You talked about how we had started high school dressing up for one another, trying really hard to figure out how to fit in and how to look cool," she said. "But by the end of high school, you talked about how we were comfortable with ourselves, and we all started to wear sweatpants and T-shirts to school, like we did when we were little kids on the playground."

I laughed. She was right. What I'd been trying to express was how much we'd grown together in those four years—and how much we'd become ourselves. At the time, though, we were all jittery and excited to graduate, just trying to get through to the celebrations, to summer, and on to our futures. I was impressed and sort of flattered that she remembered it.

"You have a real ability to impact people in a positive way," Jen added sincerely. "I don't want you to ever forget that. I think about your speech all the time."

I was touched. It occurred to me that Jen remembered me as my high school self—the person I had been all those years ago. Someone who was charismatic, secure, unburdened. It was as if Jen held up a mirror to me, and I saw myself in a way I hadn't in a long time. Was I still that person now?

I got the impression that, to Jen, the fact that I'd managed to get Fred out of Afghanistan wasn't surprising at all. In high school, I bent rules, I found loopholes, and along the way, I made friends with everyone I met. I thrived when I was making people feel comfortable and making people laugh.

In the marines, there was no rule bending. That's what I'd wanted, and that's what I'd gotten. There was time for laughter, sure, but in many ways, going to Afghanistan knocked the wind out of me. Sometimes I felt like I was still catching my breath.

When I first encountered Fred, though, and ever since then, he had a way of reminding me of the little kid inside me. It was a thing only a dog could do. Fred was naturally confident and carefree. He lived in the moment. He even looked like he was smiling. After we both came home, he helped restore those qualities in me at a time when it was especially difficult. It didn't happen all the time or all at once, but in little moments. I couldn't always see it, but that night, Jen reminded me. I was grateful.

When our time in L.A. came to a close, Josh, Fred, and I put the Pacific Ocean on our left and headed north up the coast. After ten days in one place, it felt almost as if we were starting a new road trip altogether, and we were excited for what lay ahead. As the city faded behind us, we wound along the Pacific Coast Highway, in awe of the view. The water was stunningly blue, and the cool ocean air rolled up over the bluffs and poured into the truck's open windows. We listened to feel-good tunes, songs by Weezer and Biggie Smalls and Van Morrison.

Josh and I had researched a hike in the Los Padres National Forest that would take us deep into the wilderness. We planned to spend two nights in the woods, exploring hidden hot springs and creeks. To get to them, though, we'd have to cover extremely challenging terrain under full pack weight. Josh was up for the adventure; I hoped his prosthetic would be, too. It was our first overnight hike of the trip, something we were both looking forward to.

The trail into the forest began with a series of grueling switchbacks. Heading straight up the mountainside, the steep ascent had us out of breath quickly. Overhead, towering redwoods reached for the sky, blocking most of the sun but also preventing the ocean breeze from circulating. The trail was hot. Without saying much, we pressed on, our packs creaking on our backs and Fred panting at my heels.

After an hour or so, we reached the summit. Propping ourselves up against a boulder, we rested the weight of our packs on its surface while Fred found a cool spot under a clump of bushes. High on the ridgeline, we took in the view: a vast piney wilderness to our east and the glittering Pacific Ocean to our west. The cool sea air reached us again, rushing up the mountainside and washing over us. Looking down, we could see the trail we'd just traveled in its entirety. What had only been visible in short, uphill segments on the ascent revealed itself to be a long, zigzagging path etched into the mountainside.

The next few miles covered flat ground and went by with relative ease. Josh's prosthetic had survived what we hoped had been the most challenging part of our hike. Back in the parking lot, before we began our ascent, a few hikers coming off the trail had told us the hot springs were overcrowded and campsites were hard to come by. They tipped us off to a different spot—a quiet, tucked-away area with a beautiful stream running through it—and we marked it on our map. When we came to the junction that they described, we decided the freshwater creek sounded much more appealing than battling for space at the hot springs. A trail sign pointed the way down a well-worn path toward the hot springs. But just to the left of it, we could see another, unmarked trail that had been cut through the thick brush—it was the one our friends had mentioned.

Josh eyed the trail apprehensively.

"Downhill will be tough for me right now, man," he said.

His prosthetic knee contained oil that greased the hydraulic and, just like motor oil, it became thin and lost its viscosity as it heated. After a few hours of intense hiking in the heat, Josh felt like the knee was starting to give out every so often. It's one thing to trip and fall on a trail, but it's another to be carrying a heavy pack with a prosthetic, never knowing if your leg might buckle under the weight of your next step.

"My knee is red hot," Josh said apologetically as he reached down and touched the metal beneath the plastic protective cover on the knee.

"We can go as slow as we need to," I said with optimism. "We have plenty of light left. I won't leave you behind."

As if on cue, a young couple came bounding down the trail from the hot springs. I could hear music blaring from their headphones, and they almost didn't see us as they came around the corner with their heads down.

"Oh, hey! You guys heading to the hot springs?" the guy asked when he finally noticed us, pulling his headphones back off one ear while the music continued pumping out.

"Oh, yeah," I said. "Lots of people out there?"

"It's a popular spot for sure. You guys will have fun," he said. The woman he was with couldn't be bothered; she was already up ahead, rounding the next bend. The man nodded at us, placed his oversize headphone back over his ear, and went on his way.

Josh and I looked at one another and shook our heads.

"Let's go, man. I'll slide down the hill on my ass if I have to," Josh said with a groan, getting to his feet. We hadn't come all this way to share an overcrowded campsite with a bunch of noisy vacationers.

"That's my boy!" I said. I picked up Fred's leash and the three of us walked into the woods, heading down the unmarked trail.

The trail led us back down the other side of the ridge in a steep descent through thick brush. Soon I wasn't sure if we were even on a trail. All the elevation we'd gained on our climb up the switchbacks disappeared at a rapid rate. I did my best to hide my concerns and forge the easiest path for us, avoiding fallen trees and sharp drops. Josh was too busy watching his footing and bracing himself for a fall if his knee gave out to realize that we weren't really on a path anymore. Fred pranced along right at my heels, not caring where we were going as long as we all stayed together.

My thighs burned and my toes hurt from crashing into the front of my boots with every step. When I gained too much ground, I stopped for a minute to wait for Josh. He wasn't talking much. I could only imagine the mental and physical challenge he was facing with each step. As the brush got thicker and the terrain got steeper, I started to worry we'd made the wrong decision.

Then I heard a low and steady babble rising from below us. I stopped to listen, wondering if it was the sound of the wind. It was like a distant ocean, but as I listened more intently, I realized the hushed gurgles were the sounds of the stream.

"You hear that, buddy?" I asked, knowing Josh could only hear pain. He stopped and looked up, the sweat dripping off his nose.

"Sounds like heaven," he said with a big grin.

After a few more yards, the trail widened, and we excitedly burst into the clearing. Before us was a wide creek, about twenty yards across, with a small waterfall cascading over rocks and the trunk of a massive fallen tree. It was beautiful. The water in front of us was shallow, so we crossed and headed up the other side of the bank. Someone had made camp there, leaving behind a fire ring of rocks and a large log, but we walked past it in hopes of finding a spot we could make our own. A few minutes later, we found a bend in the creek where the force of the water had created a small, gravelly beach. A collection of boulders in the middle of the stream created a deep pool of clear mountain water, perfect for wading into. Josh and I looked around and smiled.

"I officially declare this Man Camp," I said, letting my rucksack slide off my back and hit the ground with a thud. I sat on a log and started to untie my boots. The heat of the day and the stress of our improvised route would all be worth it once I submerged myself in water.

Josh sat on a boulder and removed his prosthetic to give his leg some air. The nub that remained on his right leg was swollen from being stuck inside the carbon socket attached to his prosthetic knee and foot.

"You go check it out, I'm right behind you," he said, waving me off with one hand and rubbing powder on his nub with the other.

When I walked onto the rocky beach in my swim trunks, Fred scampered to my side to see what I was up to. I started walking through the creek, stepping from rock to rock, and Fred followed, precariously balancing on the stones. I climbed onto a boulder and looked down into the deep, clear water, where a few large fish were swimming. I hopped off the rock and let gravity do the rest. Plunging into the cool water, I sank to the bottom. The shock of the cold woke my senses. I came to the surface and sucked in the fresh air, beaming.

Fred, part panicked and part excited, waded into the water and paddled toward me, his snout in the air.

"Hey, buddy!" I said, swimming toward my rescuer. Fred loved being in the water but much preferred it when he could touch the bottom. Both of us floated toward the bank so he could get his footing. It made me laugh to think about how Fred might be the only dog in his gene pool to have ever swum as much as he had.

"Looks cold!" Josh said from his spot on the bank. "I'm gonna jump in over there." He pointed upstream to where a massive fallen tree lay across the creek. The tree was the best way for him to get in the water. Wading in from the bank would have meant me helping him hop on one leg. From the tree trunk, he could leap on his own.

I swam over to the water beneath the tree as Josh climbed onto it. It was plenty deep at the midpoint, just beyond a couple of boulders on either side. Fred went out ahead of Josh, scurrying onto the trunk, looking from Josh to me and whimpering disapprovingly.

"It's okay, pal. It's just a little water," I said.

Josh took off his leg and scooted across. As he got closer, Fred calmed down, sitting back on his haunches as he watched Josh make his way toward him. When Josh got to the middle, he looked down at the drop, and I could tell it looked a lot more intimidating from where he sat. He was probably about fourteen feet over the water, and with the boulders infringing on the pool of water below, his margin for error was small.

"Just pop yourself off and go butt first," I said, trying to simplify it as much as I could. I swam downstream and found a

rock to sit on, out of the way. Fred scampered off the tree trunk and along the bank to join me, licking the cool water off my skin.

Then, without warning, Josh lifted himself by his arms and popped off the log. For a moment, the fall blew his hair upward and he let out a "Yip!" just before hitting the water. He stayed under as I had done, enjoying the peace. Just as the ripples were fading, he surfaced, taking in a big breath and then smiling from ear to ear.

We spent the rest of the day taking turns hopping off the fallen tree and swimming in the creek. No one came by; we were perfectly alone in the peaceful forest. As the sun began to sink, we started a fire at our campsite to keep the bugs away. For dinner, I heated up some water for our freeze-dried camp food. Chicken and rice for me and chili mac for Josh. They were like MREs, but better in quality and with far more flavor. Fred was curled up in front of the fire when he smelled the chicken. I added a scoop to his dry food and, to my surprise, he gobbled up his meal instead of burying it. He must have worked up quite an appetite playing lifeguard all day.

All three of us were exhausted. With the sun barely gone behind the horizon, Josh and I doused the fire and got ready for bed. We didn't care how early it was; we were excited about sleeping under the stars in our secluded oasis. The clear sky above showed no signs of rain, so we were able to sleep without rainflies over our tents. I crawled into my tent, and Fred followed and assumed his position curled up between my legs, his head resting on my thigh.

The next morning, Josh and I woke up well rested but sore.

Over a breakfast of oatmeal, dried fruit, and instant coffee, we decided to spend the day enjoying our campsite by the creek. We each found a spot along the water and read books. Fred hopped around the rocks and found a perfect chewing stick. He dragged it to a big, flat boulder and gnawed away in the sun. When the day got hot, I jumped into the creek to cool off, and spent the rest of the afternoon in and out of the water, relaxing and recuperating. It was perfect.

The next morning, we packed up and said good-bye to our little corner of the Los Padres Forest. We were already pushing the limits with Josh's leg. The three-day battery life was for normal day-to-day use. Our strenuous hike to the creek, plus another day walking over rocks, hardly constituted "normal."

We didn't bother finding the trail we'd come in on—it was a ways down the creek and barely even a trail. Instead, we started heading straight up the ridge from where we were, hoping we'd connect with a path near the top. The way up was rockier than I remembered. I felt nervous about Josh's leg, knowing he was working twice as hard as I was to scramble up the hill.

We pushed through the thick brush and gradually made our way up the steep mountainside. As we got higher, the canopy thinned, and we began to feel that fresh ocean air. After about a mile, our trailblazing paid off when we emerged like two mountain goats from the tree line, right where we'd seen the headphone-wearing couple two days earlier. We took a break for water, and then, from the end of his leash, Fred led us all the way back to the Land Cruiser. Exhausted, Josh and I sat on the tailgate of the truck and cracked open a beer. As a group of Boy Scouts walked through the parking lot, their youthful curiosity got the better of them, and they gaped at us—two sweaty, muddy guys on the back of a truck drinking beer at noon, while an extra leg and a dog rested nearby.

Satisfied by our adventure in the woods, we spent the rest of the week camping on the cliffs of Big Sur. Instead of hiking, we drove the Land Cruiser uphill, finding little turnoffs where we could camp and enjoy a view of the ocean from the tailgate. In the mornings, we made breakfast with the Jetboil and sipped instant coffee as we watched the sun burn off the haze on the flat, blue horizon. We spent our days driving over the mountain roads that crisscrossed the ridge. Whenever we got out to walk around, Fred would chase squirrels, and we'd look out in awe at the gorgeous view. One day, I mountain-biked while Josh walked down to the water and enjoyed the beach. At night, the sea breeze kept the bugs away, so there was no need for tents. We rolled out our sleeping mats and slept under the open sky; the bright, blinking stars were the last thing I saw each night before closing my eyes.

After a week camping in Big Sur, I was in dire need of a shower. My filthy state made me think of a special gift I'd once received from a villager in Sangin.

On one of my missions in Afghanistan, after Fred, I befriended a villager named Elias. Elias was a bread maker who lived in a small clay house that sat between our compound and the Green Zone.

"Please don't shoot into my house," he said to me and Ali one day, fearful he'd end up in the crossfire between us and the

Taliban. He was a tall, wiry man with a long nose and a slight hunch in his shoulders. His black beard was just beginning to turn white in a small patch below his lower lip. I guessed he was in his mid-thirties. Elias told us he had a wife and two children, a little boy of about five and a girl of three. He used to sell loaves of bread from his home, which was just off Highway 611. Eventually, though, the Taliban started showing up. Each day, they'd come and take everything he baked. So, like most small businesses in the village, he was forced to close his shop. Now, he occasionally sold bread but spent most of his time working in the fields.

We assured Elias we wouldn't make his home a target, and to give him peace of mind, I told him that if the Taliban ever took over his home, he should lay one of his rugs over the wall that faced our compound as a signal. The RECON marines who had deployed to Iraq told me they'd asked villagers to do the same if insurgents were inside. It was subtle, because it wasn't unusual for families to hang rugs that way for cleaning purposes.

A few days after our initial meeting, we stopped by Elias's house on a patrol. I knocked on his door. When he saw it was us, he graciously invited Ali and me inside for chai tea. We sat on a small rug in his home and spoke for a few minutes, then continued on our way.

I began meeting regularly with the bread maker. He was kind and welcoming, and I trusted him to give me information if he had it. His compound was close to ours, so we were like neighbors. Then we started to buy bread from him, and he'd give us big stacks of the warm, flat loaves—similar to naan—wrapped in cloth. Back at the compound, the RECON guys went nuts for it. All we had to eat were MREs, and the fresh bread was a luxury.

Each time I met with Elias, he'd invite Ali and me inside, boil water for chai tea, and we'd sit cross-legged across from each other on the rug on the floor. As he got more comfortable with me, he'd take my hands in his during our conversations, and sometimes even interlock his legs with mine—a sign of trust and close friendship. Even though we couldn't understand each other's language, we looked at each other when we spoke, and Ali would sit next to us and translate. I'd try to say a few words in Pashto here and there, like "please," and he would do the same with English words he knew. He called me "Craig-D," which is how all the Afghans tended to pronounce my name. The bread maker always spoke quickly and animatedly and was always smiling.

Often, I asked Elias if he'd heard anything about the Taliban, especially if we were on our way out for a patrol. Anything, even the smallest detail, that could reveal something about Taliban activity—and IED placement—was critical. Usually, though, he didn't know much, and our brief conversations were mostly about how his day was going and how his family was doing. Whether he had information or not, my philosophy was that it was important to build a positive rapport with people in the village. And, in truth, I enjoyed meeting with Elias. His friendship was important to me.

One night, the marines and I were headed out on a patrol. As we approached Elias's house, I saw him come to the door and slip out. He was barefoot, in a robe that looked like it must have been his pajamas.

"Craig-D, Craig-D!" he called, running toward me. When he reached me, he grabbed my hands.

"Mines!" he said in an urgent whisper. The hair on my arms stood up, and I nervously scanned the horizon. Elias explained that the Taliban had been in the field that day planting IEDs. They'd figured out that we cut through the fields at night on our patrols instead of using paths. Taliban members acted like they were sowing the fields when they were actually emplacing bombs.

Elias told me he could show us the way, and I trusted him. He took my hand and led me through the field, using a path he knew was safe. The patrol followed in a single file behind us, and slowly, in the darkness of the night, the bread maker led us through the field to safety.

It was a stunning act of kindness and bravery. Any villagers who assisted coalition forces were putting themselves at an enormous risk. Elias hadn't just helped us; he'd saved us.

In one of my last meetings with Elias, as Ali and I sat with him on the rug in his home, his face suddenly lit up. His whole body became jittery with excitement, and he jumped up from the rug, then returned with something in his hands.

"He has a gift for you," Ali explained. I was surprised and confused—aside from buying bread and sharing chai together, we'd never exchanged anything.

The bread maker sat across from me and held out his hands. In his palms was a crumpled white paper napkin with something small wrapped inside. Peeling back the napkin, Elias beamed as he revealed the gift: a travel-size bottle of shampoo. The label on the small green bottle was faded, but it looked like it said Pert Plus.

"For you!" Elias said, gesturing to my hair.

All three of us burst out laughing. I'd been living in the dirt for weeks. And with no mirror to speak of, I could only imagine how I must have looked at that point—not to mention how I must have smelled. Here was the bread maker— a man who probably had never had running water in his life—gently encouraging me to clean myself up. My guess was he'd gotten the shampoo in an aid drop, who knows how long ago.

I thanked Elias for his gift and used it back at the compound that same day. It was a perfect example of the kind of person he was. Time and again, the villagers I met in Afghanistan offered us whatever they could: tea, bread, conversation. Information, warmth, friendship. They had little but gave freely, hoping that soon, they could return to the life they wanted—one where they could live and work and raise their families without the constant threat of oppression. And we wanted, more than anything, to make that happen.

After coming home, I often thought about the bread maker. I'd heard from other marines that after I left the field, the intelligence collector who took my place hadn't maintained the relationship with Elias. No one was entirely sure what happened to him, but the stories suggested that he moved away. Maybe he moved to work the fields somewhere else, I thought, but I also knew Elias wouldn't have wanted to leave the big brick oven he owned for making his beloved bread. I worried he had received a night letter from the Taliban, threatening him for collaborating with us. Maybe he'd been forced to flee. It was crushing to think I'd never know.

At a gas station in the small town of Orick, we found ourselves without a plan. After camping in Big Sur, we'd spent a weekend in San Francisco, where we met up with another one of my childhood friends and celebrated the Fourth of July. Now, we were headed north to the Redwood National Forest, where we hoped to do another two-night backpacking stint, but the drive was taking longer than expected, and we were quickly losing daylight. Before pulling into the gas station, Josh thought he'd seen a sign by the road that read LAST STOP FOR 100 MILES. As I pumped gas, the two of us went over our options.

If we continued on, we would have to start our hike in the dark, a potentially dangerous situation we both wanted to avoid. We could stay put where we were, but by the looks of the town, there wasn't much around aside from the gas station and a church across the street. Josh volunteered to go into the general store attached to the gas station to talk to someone.

"I'm either gonna come out with a place for us to sleep or a fresh box of AAA batteries for our headlamps," he said, walking toward the little shop.

When the pump clicked and the Land Cruiser's tank was full, I leashed Fred and walked him around the parking lot. After a couple minutes, I heard the screen door of the shop slap against its frame and turned to see Josh walking toward us, followed by a gray-haired man in overalls.

"Hi there, sir," I said, shaking the man's hand.

"Name's Roger," he said. I guessed Roger was in his sixties. With his overalls and boots, he had a cowboy look. "Josh says you two are looking for a place to hole up for the night," he added.

"Yes, sir. Any suggestions?" I asked.

Roger was nodding his head before I finished my reply. "I work on the rodeo grounds right over there," he said, pointing across the street. "You three are welcome to pull in for the night and make camp. There are fire rings and a couple of port-a-johns. It isn't fancy, but it's the best I can do."

"That's a lot better than we could have done for ourselves," I said. "We weren't looking forward to hiking into the woods at night."

"I'd imagine not," said Roger. "If you wanna head back this way after your camping trip, we're having a rodeo in town this weekend. It'll be a good show—we have some talented riders coming in."

"Thank you, sir. We'll keep it in mind," I said, shaking Roger's hand once more. Inside the shop, we bought our provisions for the night: firewood, beef jerky, and Moon Pies.

In the large, grassy field across the street, we found the campground. Ahead of us, a mountain range rose up on the horizon, its tall pines standing stoically in the distance. A herd of cattle walked lazily through the field adjacent to ours, making their way back to the pen for the night. While we were only a few miles inland from the coast, it felt like we were a long way from the ocean. Content with our campsite, we started a fire while Fred trotted around, sniffing the grass and air curiously.

The next morning, we shook the dew from our sleeping bags and made coffee in the crisp air while Fred watched the cattle in the distance. On our way back to the road, Josh hopped out of the Land Cruiser and slipped a twenty-dollar bill and thank-you note under the door of a shack near the entrance. Feeling grateful, well rested, and well fed—from coffee and Moon Pies—we headed north toward the woods.

CHAPTER 12

Boom

Sangin was eerily quiet. Our new compound sat on the desert side of the highway, in the dusty, moonlike terrain, perched right alongside the Green Zone. We inserted at night and waited. But when the sun came up, the attack didn't.

After a few days, the Taliban still hadn't launched the kind of assault we'd seen in our first mission to Sangin. They knew where we were—there'd been a few pop shots fired at our rooftop posts, but that was it. We moved forward with our plan: to start engaging villagers and to make our presence known in the Green Zone. The first night patrol was scheduled. Instead of going out for a few hours, then returning, the new plan was to take a compound in the Green Zone and stay. For forty-eight hours, we'd hold and secure the compound, demonstrating our presence to the locals and the Taliban before returning. By aggressively encroaching on their territory, the idea was to send a clear message to the Taliban—that we were serious, prepared to confront them head-on.

As attachments with specific roles, Justin, Ysa, and I didn't need to go out with the patrol team. Justin and Ysa were a response team. The RECON marines had been trained in IED detection; each patrol had a designated metal detector marine who walked in front of the patrol, on point, sweeping for mines and IEDs. If they found something that they couldn't deal with themselves, they were to radio for EOD. But Justin and Ysa weren't the types to wait back on their heels. Their skills were unparalleled; they were IED experts. Justin and Ysa wanted to be there when they were needed, not sitting around in the dust waiting for a call.

Ali and I felt the same way. We weren't going to meet any villagers sitting behind these walls. The closer we got to the action, the better intelligence we could gather, whether through observation, talking with families, or interrogating a Taliban fighter. We all wanted to get out there and offer the most we could, so we requested to join the patrol. It was why we were here.

In the dark, we lined up and filed out of the compound into the night. Earlier that day, we'd reviewed the route: a four-mile trek to a village along the river where drone reconnaissance had spotted the Taliban.

After a few weeks off, it felt good to be back at work with the guys. We were accustomed to the challenging terrain now, and we moved swiftly through the Green Zone as a team, working our way in and out of cold canals and through dense fields of corn. Our boots groaned through the damp earth with a rhythm. This part of the Green Zone felt more compact: the plant life was thicker and lusher, and the trees grew taller. Instead of scrawny, naked branches, they reached toward the sky, thick with leaves. Everything was tight, as if the labyrinth of green were closing in on us. When we passed villages, I noticed the homes themselves were closer together, too—some even shared walls. That made me nervous, since it meant the Taliban could more easily move from one to another without being detected.

That night, after we fortified our target compound, Ysa, Justin, and I stayed on watch so the RECON guys could rest up for the action that would come in the morning. The new compound was small, with a courtyard and breezeway that led to a few rooms, but it also had an orchard with pomegranate trees in a separate garden area. The walls around the main compound were tall—at least eight feet high—but around the trees, the walls were only about half that height. It made for a good fighting position because we could stand up and shoot over if we needed to, using a couple of sandbags to help protect our heads.

Under the dark sky, the guys and I leaned up against the orchard wall and whispered in the quiet. We had these fancy binoculars that operated like our night vision goggles, and we'd take turns having a look around at the dirt paths, fields, and neighboring compounds. Above us, the machine gunner waited on a rooftop post. The night was quiet, though, and we took off our helmets and relaxed a little in the cool air.

I took the time to tell Justin and Ysa about what I'd seen in Trek Nawa and Sangin, but mostly we goofed off. Justin and I talked about Pittsburgh and I tried to bust his balls about the rivalry between the Penguins and Capitals, but he shut me down quickly by reminding me that my Capitals hadn't won a Stanley Cup—ever.

We swapped our stories, talking about where we'd come

from and! what led us here. Somehow we got started on high school. Ysa told us how he used to sneak out of the house in the middle of the night to go to his girlfriend's. Her dad had caught him there more than once, but he went on to marry her, his high school sweetheart, and now they had three little girls.

Justin had me laughing when he talked about getting drunk for the first time as a teenager in Pittsburgh. He'd been drinking Stroh's, this shitty, watery Michigan beer. I only knew what it was because my aunt Marie used to carry cans of it around in her purse wherever she went. It was all she ever drank.

I also finally told the guys the story about Fred. As I got to the part about Fred following me to the helicopter, they shook their heads and smiled. "I can't wait to meet him," Justin said. "My dog Duchess is gonna want to meet him, too," Ysa added.

After a few hours, the sky began to brighten, and the sun showed up on the horizon. We were off the clock, and we walked from the garden through an archway into the main compound. We'd stashed our gear in a room and we headed there to catch some sleep. On my way across the compound, though, I spotted something I hadn't seen in Afghanistan outside of Camp Leatherneck: a bed.

It wasn't actually much of a bed—more of a metal frame with plastic bands stretched across it, almost like an oversize pool chair. Still, it looked like a welcome change from sleeping on the ground.

"Dibs!" I said, grabbing it and pulling it into the breeze-way for shade. My boots and pants were still wet from wading through canals, so I took them off, changed into my shorts, and laid back on the little cot. It wasn't quite long enough—I propped my head against the mud wall behind me—but it was good enough. I closed my eyes and started to drift off to the sound of the lieutenant sending routine radio checks back to the compound.

Then: a force against my body like a wave on a beach. The sound of a loud crack. Darkness.

The memory is murky. In my mind, there's an image of one of the marines' hands—Garrett's—coming through dust and debris. I remember my body being lifted, moved. I remember hearing my name called.

As the fog began to clear, I realized I was now sitting against a wall, across the courtyard from where I'd been sleeping in the cot. Garrett was looking at me, asking something. "Craig. Buddy. Are you okay?"

I looked to where I'd been lying, and the ceiling of the breeze-way was now in rubble, on fire. Rocks and debris covered the ground. The sound of a firefight buzzed in the air.

Disoriented, I remember thinking something had gone wrong. An explosion. It must have been friendly fire, I thought, confused. How else would it have been so close?

Garrett looked at me and said: "Get your shit on."

I looked up. The guys were scrambling around, getting onto the walls, returning fire. It was starting to register: we were under attack. I found my stuff and put on my boots, then tried to pull on my pants. Something was very wrong. The pants wouldn't go on over my boots. I knew that I should be able to put my pants on easily, but the task had become a problem, and my brain was struggling to comprehend what to do next. Instead of taking off the boots and starting over, I pulled out my knife, leaned forward, and cut vertical slits at the bottom of my pants so they'd fit over the boots. I pulled them up and grabbed my gun. I saw Ysa and Justin on a wall and went to them. *Just do what they do,* I thought.

Later, I'd learn that a Taliban rocket had landed in our compound, directly behind the wall of the breezeway where I was sleeping, causing the whole area to collapse. Justin and Ysa said they'd felt the blast in their bodies; it left a ringing in their ears. When the guys looked at where I'd been and saw only a pile of rubble, they thought, *That's it.*

Now, everybody was returning fire on the compound where the rocket had come from. Its launch had sent a cloud of smoke into the air, so the guys knew their target. There was a pause; it became quiet. Then the Taliban opened up on us from another compound, much closer. We switched walls, returned fire. My body and mind were functioning on adrenaline. It was the first time we'd been in a battle like this, where the neighboring compounds were so close and we were all on flat ground. We were only a small platoon trying to secure a compound in a hornet's nest. The fact that they were able to land a rocket so accurately on our position was saying something. We were vulnerable.

The decision was made to call in HIMARS, a High-Mobility Artillery Rocket System, which could be fired with precise accuracy from a distance. Ours were launched from Leatherneck. The lieutenant sent the coordinates over the radio; a team back on base launched the missiles. With a crack, they shot into the air, a stream of smoke in their wake. They'd be landing within fifty meters of us—*danger close*—so we all took cover. Like lightning, the missiles came crashing down around us. The impact of the blasts washed through me like a force, sending painful pulses through my body.

After that, it got quiet. If the Taliban were still alive, they were fleeing. The corner where the rocket had landed was smoldering. I took off my gear and helmet and wiped the sweat from my head.

Doc Finn came over. We sat in the shade so he could give me a field exam.

"What's your name?" he asked.

"Craig."

He asked for my mother's name and her maiden name. I answered. Then he asked me how old I was.

"My girlfriend is twenty-eight," I said.

"Okay, but how old are you?"

"I told you," I said. "She's twenty-eight. I'm younger than her."

Finn patiently tried again. "Okay. But do you know your age?"

"I just told you!" I shouted, frustrated.

As the adrenaline faded, my head began to throb, and a contusion on the back of my skull started to swell. I felt like shit. Doc Finn had the information he needed. I wasn't right.

He radioed back to the other compound: "Grossi is fine but showing signs of head trauma. Potential routine medevac needed later."

I resisted. I'd grown up getting rocked in ice hockey games, taking falls against the wall. In my mind, I just needed a break—to sit on the bench for a while, shake it off, then I'd be fine. I didn't think it could be that bad. I looked okay. And I didn't want to leave my guys.

Meanwhile, Justin and Ysa did a postblast investigation of the impact site. They could immediately tell the rocket must have been bigger than an RPG. The pair poked around the rubble, and it didn't take long to find the culprit: a 107mm Chinese antitank rocket. Afghanistan was littered with them from the war with the Soviets. Now, the Taliban typically used them as IEDs because they didn't have a way of accurately firing them. They were huge—a few feet long—with the capability of incapacitating a tank. But since the Taliban didn't have the proper launch vehicle, all they could do was prop them up with a metal stand and hit the back with a hammer to launch them. We'd seen the rockets whizzing by during previous battles, always out of control and far off. We practically laughed at them.

Justin walked over with the rocket motor. I was in the middle of telling the corpsman I was fine when Justin put the motor in front of me. It was at least a foot long and wider than I could wrap my hand around. At the top end, the metal was warped and twisted from the explosion.

"Look at this," he said. "You're fucked up, man. You can't be as close to this as you were and not be messed up. You gotta get checked out."

He was adamant. He didn't know how I hadn't been turned into jam. Plus, the shock waves from the HIMARS would have only added to the beating my brain was taking.

Instead of staying another night and day in the Green Zone, our command decided the whole patrol would hump back to the rest of the company in the desert compound. It was dangerous for us where we were; part of the compound was in rubble, and the standoff between our position and the Taliban was too risky.

We waited for night to fall, huddled along the wall at one end of the compound. The pain pounded in my head. I started to feel like my brain was too big for my skull; the pressure was miserable. I couldn't eat; I was too nauseated. Instead, I tried to close my eyes. I dreamt a grenade floated over the wall and landed in my lap. I jolted awake, my heart racing.

Once it'd been dark for hours, we stepped off into the night. Trying to walk quickly made me realize my equilibrium was off. Each time I stepped down into a canal, or up again on a bank, I felt my balance shift, like everything was moving sideways. Using the night vision was out of the question, and with my head throbbing, I took off my helmet and strapped it to my ruck.

Justin was walking behind me in the patrol. "You okay, man?" he whispered.

"Yeah," I said sharply. I hated how I could tell the guys were keeping their eyes on me, worrying. I'd worked so hard to prove to the RECON marines that I was tough, that I could keep up, that I was valuable. Now I felt like a pile of mashed potatoes.

When we finally reached the compound, I met with the head corpsman, who agreed with Finn that I needed to be medically evacuated back to Leatherneck. Again, I tried to insist I just needed to rest, that I could stay; I'd be fine. If they sent me back to Leatherneck, would that be the end of my work in Sangin?

Justin and Ysa didn't want to hear it. They helped me pack up my stuff while I waited for the helicopter.

"Look, man, you won't be doing anyone any good out here if your brain is bleeding," said Justin.

"Yeah—you don't have the brain cells to spare," Ysa joked, stuffing my sleeping bag into my ruck.

When the helicopter touched down at Leatherneck, my commanding officer, Gomez, was waiting for me in the back of an ambulance on the airstrip. I'd only been gone a few days, but I was a mess—completely covered in dirt, with a beard coming in, wearing an unauthorized uniform. The RECON guys and I occasionally traded gear with the British Royal Marines, and I was wearing British boots and cammies. Gomez didn't care. I'm sure he could tell from the reports—and by looking at me— that I felt like hell.

We pulled up to the hospital, and I had to hand over all my gear. I gave Gomez my gun, knife, and bandolier. I hated to part with it all. What if this was it for me?

Inside, the doctor ordered an MRI, then sent me on my way to the recovery center. Reluctantly, I went.

The recovery center was run by the air force. As I walked in, a wave of air-conditioning shocked me. The lobby smelled like Otis Spunkmeyer cookies and blueberries. As I stood there, still covered in filth, I felt like the ground was moving beneath me. From behind a tall desk, I realized a pretty air force servicewoman was smiling at me.

"Hi there," she said, getting to her feet.

A jar of candy sat on the countertop, and a huge flat-screen TV hung on the wall next to a large, stainless steel fridge. Everything was pristine and cold, like a freezer. Suddenly I got the urge to vomit.

The air force worker was quick. She rushed over, followed by two others, and they led me to a bed—a real bed—with clean white sheets. I fell asleep instantly.

I don't know how long I was out for, but it must have been a while. My face had done a number on the pillow. I'd gotten mud on everything. Some brave soul had taken off my boots and put them at the end of my bed. On a chair next to me sat a shave kit with a towel and soap, as well as a fresh uniform. Mac and Sergio must have come by, leaving a bag of beef jerky and a handwritten note: "Clean yourself up, you're filthy. P.S. Glad you're not dead."

I woke up thinking of one thing: Fred.

I took a shower, shaved, and got cleaned up. I didn't feel quite like myself, but the sleep had helped. Back at my bed, I was greeted by an air force officer. With a clipboard in her arm and a cup of coffee in her hand, she leaned forward and shook my hand, introducing herself.

"Is it okay if I ask a few questions?" she asked.

From the way she was talking to me, I gathered she was sent to evaluate me to see if I was fit to continue my deployment. At this point, I was more nervous about Fred than anything else. If I couldn't convince her I was okay, I'd likely be shipped off on the next flight to recover in a military hospital in Germany, while Fred would be stuck in Afghanistan.

I put on my best performance. I didn't stop smiling the whole time we talked. I cracked jokes. She asked about my job and my life at home. I found out she'd lived in the D.C. area before, and soon enough, we were talking about the weather and beltway traffic like we were old pals.

After about forty-five minutes, there was a pause in our conversation, and the doctor looked at me. She was smart and could probably tell what I was doing. But she let me go, agreeing to sign the release form with the stipulation that I attend two weeks of physical therapy in the traumatic brain injury (TBI) clinic before returning to the field.

"You got it," I told her, grinning like a little kid.

Back at the intel office, I caught up with Sergio.

"Hey, man, Fred was not happy while you were away. I went over to DHL the day you got hit. I brought his favorite—roast beef—and he wouldn't eat it," Sergio said.

There was this 24-7 sandwich station in one of the chow halls. Before I left on my mission, we'd go late at night and grab a fistful of lunch meat and cheese for Fred. It was his favorite. After I left, Sergio kept up the routine for me, checking on the little guy at DHL and bringing him treats. But according to Sergio, Fred knew something was up.

"The DHL guys said he moped all day, too. Wouldn't play soccer," Sergio added.

I shook my head in disbelief. I'd felt it from the very beginning: Fred and I were connected. I couldn't wait to see him.

Sergio gave me the keys to the truck and I headed toward DHL. As I got close to the compound, I glanced in the rearview mirror and saw trouble: a convoy of black Suburbans was making its way up the road. It had to be a general or chief of staff getting a grand tour of Leatherneck—DHL included. It was the only facility up ahead.

Shit, I thought. I pulled over and watched as they drove into the DHL compound. Once they were inside, I jumped out of the car and ran up to the fence. I found a hole in the green sniper netting and looked through. Where Fred had been tied up, there were a few empty water bottles strewn around—makeshift chew toys—and a big hole he'd dug. But no Fred.

It looked like the general and his staff had started their tour. Tinashe emerged, clipboard in hand as always, and walked the group around, pointing to the whiteboard of scheduled shipments and to a truck with a bed full of large A/C units. I guessed this was probably some kind of capabilities brief. The general kept reaching for a handkerchief in his pocket, bringing it to his brow and dabbing the sweat.

I started to panic about Fred. He was still nowhere in sight, and I worried he might have run away. Or, if the DHL guys were hiding him somewhere, it was only a matter of time before he'd start to bark, giving himself away. Whoever this guy was receiving the tour, he was high ranking, and it was clear everybody around him was trying to impress him. If Fred got in the way now, his life would be in danger.

I was about to move to another spot to get a better view when I saw Peter step out of the office. Like Tinashe, he wore the usual DHL polo shirt tucked into khakis, and he stood upright, as if he were a little uncomfortable. Then I saw him. Fred was trotting beside Peter at the end of a leash. His big, fluffy tail was bouncing up and down and his snout was waving in the air as always. Peter, clearly trying to act as natural as possible, led Fred to a row of crates. The two slowly walked up and down the row while Fred sniffed along the bottom of each crate. At one, they paused. Peter lifted the palm of his hand, then smacked the top a few times, as if patting it. Fred looked up at him. Then, sending a little poof of dust into the air, he leapt on top of it.

I burst out laughing. I couldn't believe what I was seeing: Peter was parading Fred around, pretending he was a bomb-sniffing dog. And Fred, with his confident trot and natural curiosity, was actually making it look legit.

Before the show carried on much longer, the general seemed to have had enough. After wiping his brow again, I watched as Tinashe shook his hand, along with the other entourage members, and they returned to their SUVs and pulled away.

With the general gone, I got back into my truck and drove into the DHL lot. Inside, the workers were all celebrating their performance. Standing in a big circle, they kicked a soccer ball back and forth. Fred stood in the middle, happily chasing and yelping with glee.

I sat and watched for a minute, tears brimming in my eyes. The weight of responsibility for Fred came rushing back to me, but it didn't feel like a burden this time. Instead, it was my mission. I was resolved. No matter what had happened, and what might still happen, I was getting this dog home.

Eventually, Fred spotted me. He came flying over, kicking up a trail of dust and whimpering frantically with excitement. I was assaulted with love. He zipped around my ankles, popping up to lick my face, then burst away to run big laps around the compound.

"Wow, buddy!" I said. "So you're a bomb-sniffing soccer player now, huh?"

Tinashe stepped out of the office.

"Are you okay, my friend?" he asked. Sergio must have tipped him off about my injury the last time he was here.

"Yes," I said. "I'm all right."

Then Tinashe handed me a big manila envelope.

"What's this?" I asked.

"Fred's freedom," he answered. "You finish getting these filled out, and he'll be out of here on the next flight."

While I was away, my sister had mailed the paperwork to Sergio. He'd delivered it to Tinashe to confirm the forms were what he needed.

I leafed through them. There was the customs paperwork and the veterinary certification forms. Sarah had filled in as much as she could, but there were still a few veterinarian signatures required. There was no way I was going to be able to get them. But I knew what I had to do now. I was going to have to forge the forms. I knew it wasn't right, but I wasn't prepared to let a few pieces of paper stand in the way of Fred getting home.

Alone in my room that night, I spent hours practicing signatures of made-up veterinarians till they looked natural. I only had one shot to make the forms look official. If I screwed it up, it might be weeks before I'd receive new ones from Sarah. I meticulously filled in the missing fields, signing in all the right places with my practiced signature.

The forms complete, I sat back and took a breath. They looked good. Finally, I had Fred's ticket out. I didn't feel bad, exactly, but the weight of what I was doing kicked up a new wave of anxiety in my chest. I tapped my foot into the ground and ran my hand through my hair.

Maybe there was one other thing I could do. I went back to the truck and drove to the other side of Leatherneck to Bastion, the British side of the base. The Brits were more laid-back, I figured, and technically they were outside the U.S. military, so maybe less likely to get me in trouble. I knew they had working dogs, so I figured they must have a vet on-site.

I found their military police and security forces office and asked a guy walking through if there was a vet around. He pointed me in the direction of a building nearby. When I walked in, the room looked like a normal veterinary office back home. Steel exam tables, kennels. A woman looked up from her laptop in my direction.

I introduced myself, and this time, I didn't beat around the bush.

"I've got this stray dog," I said. I told her about Fred and how I was trying to get him home.

"I don't need your name on anything," I said. "But just for my peace of mind, could you examine him? Make sure he isn't sick with anything?"

She looked at me, a little stunned. After a short delay, she said, "Can you bring him in around seven tonight? By then it should be pretty empty around here."

I picked up Fred from DHL around dusk. It was pretty quiet on the roads; the only people out were contractors or civilians. I let Fred stick his head out the window in the passenger seat and smiled. For a moment, I let myself imagine the two of us doing this very thing back home.

The vet was there waiting for us, and Fred, of course, was a charmer. He let her pick him up and put him on one of the exam tables. She checked out his ears and teeth. He even let her do a rectal exam without freaking out.

"Where did you find this little gentleman?" she wanted to know.

I just laughed. "It's a long story."

"Well, he's totally healthy," she said. "He's young! Maybe six or seven months old. Just get him home as soon as you can, then get him neutered and vaccinated once he's there."

She even wrote a note for me on paper with British Army letterhead, stating Fred was cleared for travel. It wasn't an official document, but she thought it couldn't hurt.

Back at the DHL compound, I handed over all the paperwork to Tinashe: my new note along with the forged forms.

"Well done, my friend," he said, leafing through the pages. "I can get Fred out on the next flight. But we still need a kennel. Did you get one?"

I had been so worried about paperwork that I'd forgotten a critical part of the equation. In the back of my mind, maybe I was hoping Tinashe would be able to come up with a kennel for me. But it looked like that wasn't the case.

I told Tinashe I'd figure something out. As I stepped through the door, Peter and one of his coworkers ran up to me.

"Mr. Craig! We made something for Fred."

I looked at what was in their arms and, at first, didn't realize what it was. Then it registered: they had made a homemade crate for Fred. Using chicken wire and scrap wood from around the compound, they'd assembled a makeshift kennel.

Tinashe stuck his head out the office door. "I told them I couldn't send Fred in that thing, but they made it anyway!" he said.

I couldn't believe it. I was blown away by the gesture—more so than I could properly express. These guys barely knew me; they didn't owe me anything. And here they'd taken time out of their busy and exhausting schedules to make this contraption for Fred. And they'd already done so much by keeping him safe for me.

I thanked them as much as I could. Tinashe, though, insisted he needed an FAA-approved kennel. We all looked at each other apologetically, each of us wishing we could use the hand-built one. We were so close. Feeling defeated, I promised to come up with something soon, and I headed back to the truck once again.

The adrenaline rush that had kept me going all day was giving way to a crash. Every so often, my ears would start ringing, and walking around, I'd feel a wash of dizziness. I gripped the steering wheel and tried to think, but I came up with nothing. Dejected, I went home and fell asleep.

The next day, I racked my brain. Was there a way I could sneak into the military police compound and steal a kennel from them? That was probably the riskiest option. Maybe I could ask the nice British vet—but I really didn't want to implicate her; she'd already been so kind. I also hated the idea of attempting to order a crate online, or waiting for Sarah to send one, and risking Fred's livelihood any longer.

Each night on Leatherneck, the chow halls served a meal

we called "mid rats." It was whatever was left over from the day's meals: pancakes, lasagna, waffles, pasta, chicken. That night, I sat down with a tray of food and just stared into it, too stressed out to take a bite. I was about to give up on eating when I saw a young marine also sitting by himself on the other side of the chow hall. He was looking right at me. When we made eye contact, he waved for me to come over. He was a skinny, lanky kid with glasses. Young. I didn't recognize him, but I went over.

He introduced himself. Jenkins. A private. Then he leaned across the table and said, kind of quietly, "I know about Fred."

"What do you mean?" I asked, sizing him up.

"Come on, Sergeant. I want to help," he said.

I had nothing to lose, and Jenkins didn't exactly seem threatening. I asked him what he knew.

"You need a kennel," he said.

"Can you help, or are you just fucking with me?" I asked.

"I can get you one," he said. He was completely sincere. He told me he worked at the military police compound. He had the joyous duty of hosing crap out of the dogs' cages and scooping their chow.

"There are empty kennels everywhere," Jenkins said. "I can get you one. What's your room number?"

I told him. We shook hands, and he left. I didn't know how this kid knew about Fred, but I assumed some of Fred's biggest fans—Dave and Matt, or even the RECON guys—must have let it slip. In the marines, stories had a way of making their way around between the lower enlisted guys. The first three ranks—private, private first class, and lance corporal—probably make up almost 80 percent of the Marine Corps. Those guys have to do a lot of the tough, unglamorous work, and as a result, they watch out for each other when they can. You scratch my back; I'll scratch yours—that kind of thing. We had a nickname for it: the Lance Corporal Mafia.

Late that night, I heard a thud outside my door. When I got out of bed and tried to open it, I couldn't. I realized right away why the door was stuck: Jenkins had left the kennel right outside. I was in disbelief. He actually came through.

I pushed open the door and pulled the kennel inside. It was disassembled into a few pieces—a top and bottom portion made of tough molded plastic, and a metal gate for the front—but it was perfect.

In the morning, when Sergio woke up, I said, "Dude, this is it. Let's go!" I knew U.S.-bound flights departed every morning; Tinashe told me as soon as I got the kennel, he could get Fred out.

When Sergio and I pulled the truck into the DHL compound, I pressed into the horn and let out a few excited honks. Fred, who was on the end of his lead, recognized the black Toyota by now and stood wagging his tail. Tinashe came out of the office as Sergio and I pulled out the crate.

"You did it!" he said, laughing heartily.

None of us fully believed it was really happening. Peter and some of the DHL guys came over and helped Sergio and me put the crate together with zip ties. I put a little pillow and one of my T-shirts inside—plus some food from the chow hall—and let Fred wander in to check it out. I grabbed a black Sharpie and wrote across the top of the crate: SGT. FRED, USMC.

"Okay!" Tinashe said in approval once the crate was ready to go. "Today's the day." He walked over to the schedule board that he updated daily with the day's outgoing and incoming shipments. In the outgoing column, he wrote: "Bye to Fred, we will miss you, good boy. Love, DHL Staff."

I squatted down and held Fred's face, massaging his neck under his ears. He looked at me happily, tongue peeking out of his goofy teeth in a little pant. As usual, he looked like he was smiling. "Okay, buddy," I said. "You're going home."

I put a last piece of lunch meat in the crate and closed the gate behind Fred when he went in. Tinashe helped me lift it onto a wide, flat pallet, then we secured it in place with a few ratchet straps. Peter drove a forklift up to the pallet and gently lifted it, placing it onto the back of the flatbed truck. Fred sat in his crate looking out, still grinning, as if this were all according to plan.

"Do you want to come along?" Tinashe asked, pointing to the flight line. He was going to personally make sure Fred boarded the plane without any issues.

"Absolutely," I said.

Sergio and I hopped in Peter's truck, following behind Fred to the flight line. I still laugh to myself thinking about the view: a huge eighteen-wheeler pulling nothing behind it except a trailer with a little happy dog in a crate.

Tinashe pulled the truck onto the tarmac, where a huge white 747 was waiting. Peter and a few of the DHL guys had come along, and they jumped up on Fred's pallet for one last good-bye and a group photo.

The flight would take twenty-four hours: to Pakistan, then Bahrain, then Germany, and finally John F. Kennedy airport in

New York. Tinashe introduced me to the loadmaster so I could explain the special cargo. The loadmaster—a big guy with a firm handshake and long beard—was excited about Fred and his story.

"I'll be with him through the entire journey," he said. "I miss my dog back home, so it'll be nice to have some company. He's in good hands."

A forklift loaded pallets of cargo into a large bay at the side of the plane. We watched as it was Fred's turn. He was still sitting in his crate, totally relaxed.

"Bye, Fred!" we shouted and waved, a motley crew of dusty guys from all over the world, all devoted to this funny, sweet-hearted fur ball.

I thought of the RECON guys and how badly they had wanted Fred to make it home, too. I felt like I'd achieved something we could all be proud of—something that meant more to me than any medal or award. I still had four months left in my deployment. The last few days in the field had nearly destroyed me, and I didn't know what lay ahead. But a deep sense of peace settled over me. I took in a long breath and let it out.

The massive jet engines began to whir, and we watched the plane taxi onto the runway, then roar to life and speed away. At the end of the runway, the plane lifted into the sky and became smaller and smaller in the distance. I smiled and thought, *There goes my dog.*

CHAPTER 13

The Redwoods

It was in the humming forest of Redwood State Park, under the serene, towering trees, that Josh's leg broke.

That morning, we'd hiked seven miles into the forest. With our rucks on our backs, heavy with two days' worth of provisions, and Fred leading the way at the end of his leash, we walked into the woods. At first, the trail was wide enough that Josh and I could walk shoulder to shoulder. It was a welcome change from the grueling, bushwhacked path we'd forged the week before in Los Padres. On the wide, flat trail, for the first few miles, we moved at a brisk pace. Our footsteps fell into a rhythm, the possibility of adventure propelling us. We were so determined to move forward and move quickly that we almost didn't notice the redwoods rising around us like giants. It wasn't until the trail narrowed and then led us through a dry creek bed that we realized we were surrounded.

We stopped, the three of us standing in the shadows, looking up at the trees. The rough, wrinkled trunks were moss covered and red; our eyes followed them up, up, up to dizzying heights, till our vision blurred in a sky-high gathering of branches and leaves. Even though they were right in front of us, the redwoods' enormity was difficult to comprehend. It felt like being a little kid at your parents' party when all you can see are kneecaps. Life, it seemed, was above. Down on the ground, we were small and insignificant. To walk among their ancient presence, though, was breathtaking. I felt like I could sense the energy of the trees buzzing in the air.

We hiked almost six miles without even realizing it. Every time we came around a bend in the trail, we encountered even bigger and more beautiful trees. My neck became tired from craning to look up.

Overhead, the sky began to turn murky and gray, releasing big droplets of rain. We came to the wide, flat clearing of a dry creek bed that looked good enough for camp, and we decided to get settled in before the rain picked up. We pitched our tents, securing them into the loose gravel of the creek bed. Josh had a large camouflage tarp, and we suspended it about a foot off the ground and put our rucks underneath to keep them dry.

After we'd spent some time arranging camp, the rain stopped, as if it'd gotten off to a false start. I decided to explore with Fred while Josh took a nap in his tent. With Fred on the leash—we'd read warnings about bears and mountain lions in the area—we followed the dry creek bed through the forest, scampering over loose rocks and gravel.

About a mile up the creek, we spotted a fallen giant. The tree had to have been over two hundred feet tall. I imagined the sound it would have made when it came down: a thunderous crash, like a freight train in a blender. The tree was breathtaking, even in its death.

I picked up Fred and, keeping him tucked under my arm,

found a way to scramble up onto the trunk. Fred loved running up and down the trunks of fallen trees, and I wanted nothing more than to see him prance along the mighty redwood. Cautiously, we stood and got our bearings, then together we ran along it like two kids on a playground. With his low center of gravity, it was as if Fred were made for balancing on uneven surfaces like this. He scurried back and forth over the trunk, turning to look back at me, mouth open, ears perked, eyes wide. As soon as I ran toward him, he'd turn and run, too, tail wagging.

When we finally climbed down from the tree, we sat at its base and looked out into the woods. The afternoon sun broke through the rain clouds and warmed us up while we rested, totally at peace. In moments like that, it'd hit me all at once: here I was, standing beside a centuries-old redwood tree in California with my stray dog from Afghanistan. It seemed like we'd been destined to end up here.

Back on Camp Leatherneck, after I'd watched the plane carrying Fred take off and disappear into the distance, I called Sarah, who had been helping me all along.

"Hey, sis," I said. "Fred is on the way. He'll be at JFK in twenty-four hours. Can you and Dad—"

"We'll be there," she said, before I could finish.

I sent Sarah the flight details and waited. I was in limbo: stuck on Leatherneck, going to physical therapy, working in the intel office, wondering about Fred. I walked around the place like a ghost—empty, going through the motions, my mind somewhere else entirely.

The wait felt like an eternity. Finally, after little food or sleep, enough time had passed. It was the middle of the night. I don't remember if I'd fallen asleep and woken up again or if I'd just laid there all night. I sat up on my cot, grabbed my sat phone, and walked outside. The stars twinkled overhead. I pressed the buttons and held the phone to my ear.

It rang, then the line clicked. I heard Sarah's voice on the other end.

"We got him," she said. "He's beautiful, Craig."

I let out a choke of laughter. Tears ran down my cheeks.

"You did it," Sarah said. "You did it!"

When I called, Sarah, my dad, and Fred were in the car driving from New York City back to Virginia. Sarah told me how, at customs, both the loadmaster and pilot had come out and introduced themselves. "This is a great dog. He took a piss in Germany," the loadmaster told her.

Sarah laughed, grateful Fred had been so well taken care of. When the paperwork cleared and they finally were able to let Fred out of the kennel, he carefully stepped out, looked around at the group of people, and then walked right up to Sarah. Someone had whispered, "How did he know that's his sister?"

Our conversation was only a few minutes long, but the joy we shared over the phone that night was electric. I remember the way the tone in Sarah's voice shifted subtly before we hung up, though. She didn't say it outright, but I could hear it in her good-bye: she was saying, "You did this—but you're not done." I still needed to come home, too.

Neither of us knew it then, but the worst part of my deployment still lay ahead.

When Fred and I walked back to camp, I heard a loud thumping as we approached. It sounded like Josh was driving a stake into the ground with his hatchet. But when we came around the corner and I got a look at him, I saw he was sitting on a log, his prosthetic in his hands, slamming it against the tree. Then he paused, holding the mechanical knee up to his face to examine it.

"Hey, man. What happened?" I said.

"Some dirt found its way in and jammed up my knee," Josh said. "Stupid thing is supposed to be used in the field. I put the dust cover on and everything."

Josh explained that when he woke up from his nap, he decided to try to assemble a shelter using the tarp. If it rained some more, we could use it for cover. But when he knelt down in the creek bed to unhook the tarp from where it covered our rucks, some gravel got into the joint of his prosthetic knee. When he stood up, the leg jammed up and he lost his footing, falling onto his elbow and pushing even more gravel into the knee's exposed mechanics. Now, he was trying to clear the tiny pebbles and dirt from the joint with a small brush meant for cleaning the inside of a rifle. A trail of blood ran down his forearm from where he'd fallen on his elbow.

The whole time we'd been traveling together, I'd never seen Josh like this. Even in challenging circumstances, he was always calm. Now, though, his whole body was tense with frustration. He was bent forward over the leg, sweaty and strained, completely exasperated. I didn't even know if he realized he was bleeding. The leg was humming like an electric razor, and Josh's fingers were raw from digging at the robotic hinge of the knee. I fastened Fred's leash to a nearby tree and took a seat across from him.

CRAIG & FRED   191

"Why's it humming like that?" I asked.

"I have no fucking idea, man. I've never heard it do that before," he said as calmly as could be expected from a guy holding his own leg.

"The good news is that I got out all of the rocks and got it to stand up straight again," he added, taking a breath. "The bad news is that the knee is completely shot. Now it's essentially a really expensive peg leg."

"Okay," I said, pausing to think. Josh was just starting to get really good at taking on the uneven, treacherous trails we'd been on. It was pretty amazing that he'd trekked through the Los Padres forest on those switchbacks and through the brush without any problems, especially with the weighted pack he was carrying. Now the knee was busted just from kneeling on the ground. If I were him, I would have been pissed, too.

We didn't have many options. Josh had a backup leg in the Land Cruiser, but it wasn't charged. The only real possibility was to hike back to the truck, then go somewhere to charge the backup leg so Josh could start using it.

"What if we hike out tomorrow morning and take our time?" I said. It was already getting late in the day. "That way you don't strain your good leg."

Josh agreed, and we settled into camp for the night. We heated up our dinners and sat around our campsite until dusk. We talked about the faulty mechanics of the knee and how Josh planned to call one of the reps from the manufacturer with suggestions so the same problem wouldn't happen to anyone else. As it started to get dark, Fred and I took another walk to hang our food from a tree, out of reach from curious wildlife. When we came back, Josh had already climbed into his tent, exhausted from the physical strain of the hike and the mental frustration of being betrayed by his leg.

That night, another storm rolled in. The thick canopy above protected us from the downpour. Light drops of rain pitter-pattered against the tent. Fred and I lay safe and dry under a blanket of cool mist, and the rain sang us to sleep.

When the morning sun filtered through the ancient giant trees, the sunlight warmed the inside of the tent just enough to wake us. Outside, Josh fiddled with his leg while Fred and I went to retrieve the food I'd strung up the night before. Inside the bag was our precious Jetboil and a jar of instant coffee. As I approached the spot, I was shocked to see that the dirt beneath the suspended bag looked disturbed. I crouched and got a closer look, and there they were: huge paw prints. I could see where the creature—I guessed a bear—had circled under the bag. Right beneath it, the soil was torn up even further where it must have stood on its hind legs trying to reach our stash. Fred looked as if he were vacuuming the whole area with his nose—snout to the ground, he paced across the divots of earth. Meanwhile, I untied the knot from around the trunk of the tree and let the bag fall to the ground. It had been untouched but not unnoticed. See-ing the paw prints, I was glad that Josh's leg gave us a reason to leave. We were not the biggest creatures in the forest.

When we got back to camp, Josh was too focused on adjust-ing to his leg not bracing under his weight to care much about the bear tracks. The six-mile hike back to the truck was going to be unpleasant. He knew it'd hurt.

"Just go, man," he said, our rucks on our backs. He didn't want to feel like he was holding me up.

"Listen, there's no rush. I'll go in front. If you start to go down, try to fall forward onto my ruck so you can catch your-self," I said.

We stepped onto the trail. Almost immediately, it seemed more challenging than it had on the way in. The rain had turned the red soil to mud and left the rocks on the trail slick. Every slight rise or fall in the path seemed treacherous now that Josh was essentially hiking with one leg. At any given moment, his prosthetic knee could give out if he put too much weight on it. I did my best to keep an even pace, pausing every so often to check on Josh while also trying not to burden him with my concern. Fred could tell something wasn't quite right. Once in a while, he'd stop to sniff something, then he'd lift his head and look back at Josh, who was quiet with concentration, focusing completely on staying on his feet.

When we at last reached the creek crossing, we knew there was only a mile left to go. Josh picked up the pace, even passing Fred and me in a combination of determination and frustration. He hadn't fallen yet, and I knew he couldn't wait to get to the Land Cruiser and take off his useless leg.

At the end of the trail, Fred and I caught up to him and, together, the three of us walked out of the redwoods, the same way we'd come in. We got to the Land Cruiser, and I dropped the tailgate as fast as I could so Josh could get off his feet. He took a seat and removed his leg while I poured Fred a big bowl of cool water from the cooler. We'd made it.

After driving a few hours north from the redwoods, into Oregon, it probably shouldn't have come as a surprise to us that when we first pulled up to the campsite we were aiming for—

one with electricity—we were told it was full. Doing my best to hide my frustration from the park ranger, who was just doing her job, I'd asked, "Would you be kind enough to point us to a coffee shop or bar where my friend here can charge his leg?"

Patiently, she'd smiled and said, "Go to the Blue Moon. Best wings in town, and their outlets work, too."

The Blue Moon Saloon and Cafe in Coos Bay, Oregon, was our favorite kind of bar: a dive. Josh and I walked in and grabbed two seats at the far end of the bar—a spot beside an outlet where Josh plugged in the backup leg. It was about three in the afternoon and no one was around yet. But we could tell from the advertised beer-and-a-shot happy hour and the kara-oke machine in the corner that the place could become lively.

After an hour of nursing a few beers and eating sandwiches and Utz chips that came in plastic baskets, Josh's leg was slowly booting up. Still, it was taking a while. The thing had three little LED lights that needed to go from blinking to solid green before it would be good to go, and the first light was still blink-ing. Our next planned destination was Crater Lake, a few hours east, but it was clear we'd need to find a place to stay in Coos Bay for the night. The problem was, Josh and I were starting to run low on cash. We pulled out our phones and searched for another campground, but neither of us was having any luck. Eventually, we gave up, figuring we'd find a cheap hotel that night. I tried not to worry about our shrinking budget.

Around five o'clock, the bar came to life as the local watering hole. The crowd was mostly guys—some our age, some older. They came in wearing flannel shirts and Carhartt pants with work gloves stuffed into their pockets. Budweisers and shots of whiskey were the drinks of choice, and everybody seemed to know each other.

A woman in jeans, boots, and a flannel shirt pulled up a stool near us and ordered two beers. She waited with the cool glasses in front of her, drinking one of them while keeping an eye on the door. Since it looked like Josh and I were going to be here awhile, I decided to strike up a conversation, see if she knew of a nearby campground.

"You having a two-beer kinda day?" I asked. It was the best icebreaker I could come up with.

She shot me a quick look and said, "Somebody's meeting me after work." Then she added: "Though if he doesn't get here soon it'll just be two empty glasses."

I smiled. "You wouldn't happen to know if there's another campground nearby, aside from the one outside of town, would you?"

"Unfortunately, that's the only one," she said. "You two just passing through?"

I introduced us the way I usually did, as two veterans taking the summer to drive across the country, showing my Afghan dog America. I pointed to the Land Cruiser, parked just outside the window, where Fred was resting his head on the doorframe, taking in the sights and smells of Coos Bay. It was a cool day with a fresh ocean breeze coming in off the coast, and Fred looked happy as ever in his prime people-watching spot.

The woman glanced from Fred to me, smiling. "I'm Ashley," she said, extending her hand to shake ours. As we talked, the bar continued to fill up. People who came in alone were instantly welcomed by the fellow patrons. Most didn't even have to order a beer; the once sleepy bartender had sprung to life and was opening bottles and pouring shots for everyone who came in—he already knew everybody's orders. A bearded guy in a hoodie and baseball cap walked in and, spotting Ashley, came over to us.

With a firm handshake, he introduced himself as Chris. "When Ashley texted and told me she was talking to two veterans at the bar, I assumed it was two old guys, not you two handsome bastards," he said, and Josh and I laughed.

"So, what brings you guys into our little town? Is this a stop on the run-down-town tour?" Chris joked.

"We heard you guys had the best electricity in Oregon," Josh quipped, looking over his shoulder at his prosthetic leg leaned up against the wall. By now, two of the lights were solid green.

"Whoa!" said Chris in what appeared to be genuine shock. "That looks like something out of *The Terminator*!"

Ashley playfully smacked him on the back, nearly knocking his dingy ball cap off his head and spilling some of his beer. She started to apologize to Josh, but we were laughing too hard to care. The four of us continued to joke and talk. We learned Ashley handled billing and orders for a local logging company while Chris worked half the year in fishing and the other half in logging. Josh and I told them about our road trip so far.

"Well, your experience in the redwoods explains why you both smell like bear farts," Chris said, receiving another smack from Ashley.

"What he means to say is that if you two want to, you're more than welcome to stay the night at my place. You can do laundry in the morning and get cleaned up. I don't have much, but I'd love to have you," Ashley offered.

Josh and I were stunned. We'd resigned ourselves to finding a patch of woods or motel room to spend the night in, but the thought of doing laundry and sleeping indoors was pretty appealing at this point. We'd run out of friends to stay with until we got to Seattle, where we planned to crash with one of Josh's buddies from the army.

I tried to politely protest, but Ashley quickly shut me up.

"My two boys are with their father this weekend, so I have room. You can sleep in our camper—that's where they like to play, so you'll just have to excuse the mess. This is really all for Fred, anyway. I can't wait to meet him and spoil him," she said, looking back out the window toward the Land Cruiser.

Instead of carefully watching the LED lights on Josh's leg, waiting for it to charge, we sat back and enjoyed spending the rest of the night with new friends.

Later that night, with the cool coastal air gently blowing through the open windows of the camper, we slept like the dead. The space felt luxurious, especially compared to our tents. I'd crawled my way up onto a loft bed, Josh took the bed in the back, and Fred lay on a couch seat. The whole night, I don't think one of us so much as stirred. In the morning, I awoke to the squeal of the door as it opened. Ashley pressed her fingers to her lips as she crept in. "Just grabbing your laundry," she whispered. "Breakfast will be ready in an hour, sleepyheads."

Ashley was being so generous, it was almost embarrassing. I didn't know how we'd repay her for her hospitality. It wasn't long after she came in for our clothes that the smell of bacon wafted into the camper from Ashley's kitchen window. Her home was a single-story ranch on a big stretch of land. A long gravel driveway led to the house, and out back, there was a big deck and, beyond it, a chicken coop. Dirt bike trails created by Ashley's sons stretched from the house back through the woods. The camper sat next to the house, on the other side of the driveway. As Ashley warned, it was obvious the kids loved to play inside. There were toy trucks and guns scattered about on every surface.

When we got up and walked into the kitchen, we found Ashley buzzing around, flipping bacon and pulling hot toast from a toaster at the same time, tossing each piece of perfectly browned bread onto a plate. "Have a seat!" she said cheerfully, and we sat down obediently in front of fresh mugs of coffee.

In a small porcelain bowl, Ashley mixed together some rice, eggs, and bacon for Fred. She knelt and placed it in front of him, rubbing his ears while he sniffed his special breakfast, preparing to devour it. Then she stood and slid our plates in front of us: bacon, eggs, toast, and home fries, along with her special homemade hot sauce. Up until that point, I held myself in high regard when it came to my breakfast-making skills, but I realized that I had a lot to learn if I ever wanted to make anything as good as what Ashley put in front of us. It was delicious.

We spent the day walking around Coos Bay together. Ashley and Chris took us to the best seafood place in town, and we shared one last beer together at the Blue Moon. Josh and I had decided that we'd gather our things from Ashley's place when we got back and head to a beach to camp. We were overwhelmed by Chris and Ashley's kindness and didn't want to overstay our welcome, despite their insistence that we weren't.

Back at the house, Josh and I packed up the Land Cruiser

while Fred circled our feet. Ashley walked over with two plastic shopping bags and set them down on the tailgate.

"Now you two aren't gonna leave here without this, and I won't take no for an answer," she said.

From one of the bags, she reached in and lifted out a mason jar to show us.

"Chris caught this tuna a few months ago. I cooked it and canned it on the spot. It's better than anything you two are gonna eat on the road and certainly better than any store-bought crap," she said. "I added a box of saltines and a bottle of my homemade hot sauce in there for you, too."

She pulled out each item as she mentioned it, as if to prove she meant what she said. Then, with everything back in its place, she tied the bag shut. From the second bag, she pulled out something I could honestly say I'd never seen before.

"These are firebugs," she said. "I made a bunch for my boys' Scout troop but they didn't use 'em all. Place it in the middle of some dry kindling and it'll get your fire going."

I tried not to act too impressed but I couldn't help it. The firebugs were genius. To make them, Ashley had taken the bottom of a cardboard egg carton and cut it into individual pieces. Then she'd filled each socket with wood shavings from the sawmill where she worked and sealed them off by dripping candle wax over each one. Each firebug was like a small, pocket-size fire starter.

"These will burn forever!" I said, taking one from the bag in total fascination.

"We thought we were seasoned campers by now, but you just put us in our place," Josh added. Like me, he picked one up and examined it. "I bet you could light a fire in the rain with one of these."

Ashley chuckled at our amusement, then pulled us in for hugs. We were grateful for the gifts, but I knew the big thing we'd take away from our time with Ashley and Chris was the immeasurable nature of their kindness. Without asking anything in return—without even knowing much about us—they'd taken us in and taken care of us.

"Hold my leg," Josh said, looking back at me with a cocky smirk.

The two of us stood on a cliff overlooking Crater Lake. Fred, a little wary, stood behind us, keeping an eye on our every move. The bright blue, cloudless sky overhead matched the surface of the water below. At about twenty feet high, well above the deep water below, the cliff was safe to jump from. Still, Josh would need to make sure he vaulted his body far enough out to avoid getting snagged by the cliff side on the way down. It was not at all the same as dropping in off a log, as we'd done in Los Padres.

Arriving at the dazzling azure lake was our reward after a long day. That morning, Fred and I awoke in our tent to the strangest sensation. The ground beneath us felt as though it was vibrating, and the taut plastic walls of the tent shook ever so slightly, back and forth like a square of Jell-O. Fred looked at me with a confused expression, his eyebrows lifted and head tilted. After a few seconds, I realized what we were feeling: an earthquake. I'd experienced a few before, back while I was training in California, but they were quicker and more violent. This one seemed to continue for almost a minute, as if gently lulling us out of our sleep.

Once it had run its course, we emerged from our tent and discovered that it'd snowed overnight. A dusting of the fluffy white stuff covered the ground. The whole morning made me feel as if I'd dreamed up the surreal, beautiful landscape.

Josh, Fred, and I spent the day hiking around the lake. The trails were challenging. The more we climbed, the hotter it got, making the mysterious morning snowfall seem like it must have been a hallucination. After hours of exploring over twelve miles of the area, we'd saved the best hike of the day for last: a mile stretch straight down to the water's edge. All day, Josh had been doing great on his well-charged backup leg. We moved at a good clip, and we were having so much fun, I almost forgot about the long, intense struggle of the redwoods. If he was in any pain, he didn't say anything. We took on a grueling series of switchbacks and, at last, made our way down.

On the cliff, Josh sat down and popped off his prosthetic. A crowd of people stood nearby watching people jump. Once Josh removed his leg, they couldn't help but stand agape as he balanced precariously at the edge. I knelt down on all fours beside him so he could reach down and use my back for balance, then propel himself forward. I felt Josh's cold, dry hand on my shoulder, and I looked down at the water below. I was about to ask if he wanted me to count down when, without warning, Josh launched himself up and out.

I watched as he sailed through the air, leg first, arms out, in total freefall. When he hit the water, he slipped deep beneath its smooth, reflective surface with a splash.

When Josh reappeared, blowing out a mouthful of water and smiling widely, everybody around us erupted in cheers. I looked around, confused and impressed. There was even a woman who looked like she was in tears. I hadn't realized till then just how closely the crowd was watching us. Fred clambered down the rocks to meet Josh at the bottom, making sure he was okay. I followed behind, Josh's prosthetic in hand, smiling.

CHAPTER 14

The Mud Fields

I was miserable on Leatherneck. I did my two weeks of physical therapy at the TBI clinic and was cleared to go back out into the field, but I needed to wait. The RECON guys I'd worked with from the beginning were still back at the compound I'd been medevaced from, but they were coming to the end of their deployment. In another couple of weeks, they'd all be back at Leatherneck and a new company of RECON marines would take their place. When the new company inserted, I'd go out with them.

It felt good to hang out with Sergio and Mac, to eat real food and work out in the gym, but I wanted to be back in the dirt with my guys. Too much time in the air-conditioning drove me nuts. Physically, I was doing okay. I still got dizzy if I stood up too fast or if I worked out too hard. At night, I got headaches. But I wasn't telling anyone about that. With Operation Fred accomplished, my focus was getting back out into the field. Even though the RECON marines were leaving, my EOD buddies, Justin and Ysa, were staying out there. I couldn't wait to see them and let them know Fred had made it home.

Right before I returned to Sangin, I received a package in the mail. When I opened it, I found a small photo album, assembled and sent by my sister. In it were pictures of Fred: sitting in the back of the car on the way home from the airport; sopping wet and confused during his first bath; hanging out on the couch with my dad; rolling in the grass and drinking from a fountain in the backyard of my childhood home. I turned the pages over and over again, staring at the pictures. I fell asleep looking at them. Seeing that Fred was really back home made it all feel real for the first time.

Finally, after nearly a month on Leatherneck, I reinserted by helicopter, just as I had all the times before. When the new RECON guys and I reached the compound, it was as if I'd never left. I walked up to the little room Justin, Ysa, and I had initially claimed, and there they were, half-asleep, their mats in the same spots as before. The corner where I'd had my sleeping mat and stuff was clear, as if they'd saved it for me.

I walked in and dropped my stuff, saying, "What did I miss?"

"Look who's back from the 107 party," Ysa teased, referring to the 107mm rocket that'd nearly killed me.

"You didn't miss much," Justin said. "Couple gunfights and a few episodes of *Breaking Bad*."

The guys got up and hugged me. Their beards were coming in strong and so was their body odor. I could tell Justin—who had found the rocket in the postblast evaluation—seemed a little surprised I was back out in the field. He asked how I was doing, but he didn't push it.

"How was the ice cream back on Leatherneck?" Ysa asked,

making a reference to Forrest Gump's relaxing recovery after he got shot in the butt.

"Oh, it was delicious," I said. "I got Fred out, too."

I told the guys the whole story. They couldn't believe it.

"Man, you got scammed," Ysa said. "That dog's actually a Taliban sleeper agent. Now he's gonna go back and infiltrate our government. He'll hold your dad hostage."

The teasing was endless. It was what we did. Next time I took a shit, Ysa said, "Here you are shitting in a bag while your dog is back home eating cheese and sleeping in your bed." I laughed, and Justin just smiled and shook his head.

Over the next few days, we stayed in the compound, and the new RECON team got familiar with the terrain. By the fourth night, we were headed out on a patrol. The plan was similar to the last one: we were going into the Green Zone to take a compound. We'd hold it for a few days, right in the heart of Taliban territory. And just as we'd done before, Justin, Ysa, and I chose to go.

The night started out like all the others. We ducked through the doorway of our compound, out into the cool, dark desert, and headed toward the lush fields and canals of the Green Zone. It felt good to be back to work, and I fell right back into our routine. We slipped down the ridge, crossed the first canal, and headed into a dense field of corn.

It was in the second field that we realized something was wrong. By the time the point man was about halfway through it, he'd sunk hip-deep in rich, dark soil. The field was flooded.

We didn't have any other choice; we waded into the slop. It was dense, almost like chocolate pudding. With each step

I took, I moved just inches forward, and the mud pulled me down. What should have taken a few minutes was taking nearly an hour. Finally, a few of us made it to a berm on the opposite side. Justin passed his canteen around, along with a Clif Bar from one of his wife's care packages.

When I looked back into the field, I saw the machine gunner—a young guy who must've been carrying his weight in gear—thrashing in the mud, quietly sinking. I left my pack with Justin and Ysa on the berm and waded over to him, taking his gun to lighten his load.

Eventually, the rest of the patrol made its way through. One of the marines lost his boot in the sucking mud. He frantically tried to recover it, but we didn't have the time.

When we got to the next field, it too was flooded, and so was the one after it. A patrol that should have only taken us a few hours took nearly all night. When we finally arrived at the compound, we were exhausted, and we only had an hour or two to go until sunup. We told the RECON guys to get rest while they could, and Justin, Ysa, a marine named Brian, and I got to work filling sandbags.

The compound was pretty small, but its walls were high. We dug out murder holes and fortified a rooftop post on top of one of the rooms. One of the doorways didn't have a door, so we also filled enough sandbags to block it.

By sunup, the compound was in good enough shape. Justin, Ysa, and I found an empty room and collapsed. We took off our boots and tried our best to get warm and dry. We were caked in mud from the waist down, and it was smeared on our faces, chests, and hands. We laid our sleeping mats side by side and lay close together to try to share body heat. I could tell Justin, who was in the middle, couldn't get comfortable. I even thought I heard his teeth chattering. From my ruck I pulled out an extra pair of wool socks and gave them to him. (Any time anyone back home asked me what I needed in a care package, I always asked for three things: beef jerky, instant coffee, and wool socks.)

"Thanks, man," Justin said, putting them on. For a short time, we slept.

A few hours later, the attack came. When we woke up, the radio was buzzing, and marines were scrambling to get on a wall. Immediately, the fire was rapid, constant, and accurate. The rounds sounded closer than I'd ever heard. I worried that, once again, our standoff—the space between us and them—was too narrow. Sean, the gunner who had been on the rooftop post all morning, was at the end of his shift but wouldn't come down. He was a skilled machine gunner and had already taken out a group of Taliban fighters, but he knew it was still going to get ugly. The RECON guys remembered Sean telling them: "You can come up, but I'm not coming down. You guys will want me up here in a few minutes anyway." Missenheim, another marine, got up there and joined him.

Justin, Ysa, and I got on the wall. In this kind of attack, we were marines first, EOD technicians and intelligence collectors second. Through the hole, I could see a narrow alley and the wall of the neighboring compound less than twenty feet away. Above us, on the roof, Sean was peeking his head above the sandbags, trying to get a visual on where the fire was coming from. How many fighters, which weapons, where they were.

The more we knew, the more accurately we could engage them and take them out.

But then, a loud shout came from the roof.

"Corpsman!"

My heart rattled against my chest and I turned my head to see. I heard it again, an urgent cry: "Corpsman!"

The shouting was coming from Missenheim, the teammate who had joined Sean on the roof when he didn't come down. Their position was being overrun with gunfire. Sean was shot.

I ran over. He'd been hit right under the brim of his helmet, in his forehead, and Missenheim was trying to stop the bleeding on the roof. But we needed to get him down. Bullets were buzzing directly overhead, some hitting the small sandbag barrier in front of them.

The corpsman, Doc Jones, found a rope and threw it up to Missenheim. He lassoed it across Sean's chest, under his arms, and started to lower him down. As his body came over the edge of the roof, we heard him suck in a deep gasp of air. He was still alive.

I recognized Sean from when we'd gathered on the tarmac before our departure, just a few days earlier. Some of the new RECON guys had heard about Fred and were asking about him, Sean included. I remembered the way he'd smiled and laughed heartily. He had blond hair and a big, Viking-like frame. He looked young—maybe just twenty years old—but I got the feeling he was an old soul.

Doc and I grabbed Sean and guided him down onto a litter—a small tarp stretcher—on the ground. The lieutenant had already begun to call for a medical evacuation over the radio.

We quickly wrapped Sean's head with gauze and inserted an IV. His blood pressure was dropping and his breath was shallow. I helped Doc Jones start a tracheotomy. We wiped Sean's neck with alcohol and I put my hands on his throat, right above his collarbone, holding the skin taut while Doc made the incision. Into the hollow of Sean's windpipe, he inserted the tube to release air, and I started to help him breathe while Doc Jones continued to monitor his vitals, radioing his status to the approaching medevac team. Beside us, Sean's helmet lay faceup to the sky, a pool of blood, tissue, and skull inside.

I watched Sean breathe; he was still doing it on his own. I'd give him two breaths, then he'd give one. He was unconscious, but in case he could still hear, I talked to him. "You're gonna be okay, man. You're a badass. Stay with us."

I felt like my hearing was heightened. The echoing, tinny sounds of the ongoing firefight enveloped me. I heard the strained, unfamiliar voices of marines saying, "Stay here, Sean. We need you. Don't go. Don't go." The repeated *pop-pop-pop-pop-pop* of machine gun fire overhead as Missenheim continued to work from the roof. The numbers Doc Jones spat rapidly into his radio. And finally, the steady *thump-thump-thump* of the medevac in the distance.

As the firefight continued around us, two RPGs flew overhead, landing inside our compound. They landed with a sharp, explosive crack, sending rocks and debris erupting into the air, but no one was hurt.

The incoming medevac was an air force team called Pedro. They always came in twos: one bird was armed to the teeth and would come in first to provide security for the second bird.

The second one was an airborne ambulance; it held the medical crew. They were the ones who would need to make the perilous landing in the middle of the firefight to get Sean.

Overhead, we saw the armed helicopter come in fast and low, spraying machine gun fire into the Taliban-occupied compounds. Close behind, the second bird began to descend over us, trying to come down in the compound. I looked up and saw bullets ricochet off its belly.

Over the radio, the pilot said, "There's not enough space to land!" And we watched as he pulled the helicopter up. But in the next second, he rotated it almost 360 degrees and zipped to the other side of the compound, toward an open field. The maneuver was quick, almost like a barrel roll.

"Fuck it," I heard the pilot say over the radio. "We're putting it down."

He'd decided to land the only place he could—in the adjacent field, where they'd be completely exposed.

We needed to move fast. With a count of three, Justin, Ysa, Brian, the radio guy, and I picked up Sean on the litter and sprinted toward the doorway. But it was blocked, filled from top to bottom with sandbags that we'd filled the night before. Now they needed to come down, fast. We put Sean down and rushed to the door, scrambling to yank bag after bag away from the entrance. The longer the helicopter was on the ground, the more time the Taliban had to ready another RPG. From the roof, Missenheim continued to lay down fire, providing as much cover as possible so we could safely get Sean to the helicopter.

We tore at the sandbags. From between them, I saw a blue

hand reach through from the other side. It was the gloved hand of the pararescueman, a PJ, as they're called. He'd jumped out of the helicopter to help us clear the doorway—something well above and beyond his duty, maybe even against orders.

With enough room cleared, we picked up Sean on the litter and rushed into the field, making our way toward the open door on the side of the medevac. One of the two pilots had gotten out and was shooting toward the Taliban with his pistol. The PJ who'd helped clear the doorway fired his rifle, covering us as we ran.

When we got to the helicopter, we lifted Sean inside, and Doc Jones shouted out a final round of vitals as the pilot and PJ jumped in. The bird sprung from the ground immediately, Sean's huge boots still hanging out the side as it ascended into the sky. Despite the severity of the situation, we couldn't help but smile at that, seeing our Viking buddy almost too big to fit in the helicopter.

Missenheim screamed at us from the roof to get back in. It would've been easy to take us all out with one spray of machine gun fire. We ran for our lives. Right before I passed through the doorway back into the compound, I looked up at Missenheim just as a round struck him in his vest. Dust flew off his body armor, but he barely flinched. He was pissed. We all were.

Back in the compound, it was as if the Taliban could smell blood. They knew they'd gotten one of us, and it emboldened them. I wasn't just hearing bullets whiz by; I heard the actual AKs being fired and Taliban fighters shouting to each other. They were right there. I got on a murder hole and fired out. In my four months in Afghanistan, I never saw the enemy like this.

Holy shit. We're gonna get overrun, I thought. Videos I'd seen of Taliban fighters overtaking coalition forces flashed in my mind. I pictured them standing over stolen gear and stripped, mutilated bodies. *No. That's not how my family is gonna see me.*

A 107 rocket whizzed overhead and sputtered into the distance.

"Hey—nobody take that; that's Craig's!" Ysa shouted. I looked over and saw him against the wall like me, smiling like a Cheshire cat. I couldn't help but laugh.

At last, HIMARS were on the way. It was impossible to say how long we'd been fighting, but it felt like hours. With the rockets incoming, we took cover. We lay on the ground, faces in the dirt, with our hands over our heads.

After the blasts, it was quiet.

No one had much to say. We didn't know if Sean was going to make it, and no news had come in over the radio. We wanted to give the RECON guys some space. That was their friend they'd just watched get medevaced out. They took inventory on their ammo while Justin and Ysa went over to the lieutenant and radioed our base—the other compound—to give them an update.

I stood in the courtyard with Sean's blood on my boots and uniform, unsure what to do. I wanted to scream. I wanted to kill something. I spotted some baby chicks wandering around the compound. I picked one up, feeling the gentle prickle of its feet and soft down of its feathers against my palm. Justin and Ysa came over, and we sat down to eat something. I fired up my Jetboil to heat the MREs, and we joked we were going to make a meal out of the chick. But instead we gently passed the little thing between us, smiling and taking pictures.

Craig and Fred in Afghanistan. *(Courtesy of Dave Moran)*

Fred napping in Afghanistan. *(Courtesy of Craig Grossi)*

Car and driver nap. *(Courtesy of Craig Grossi)*

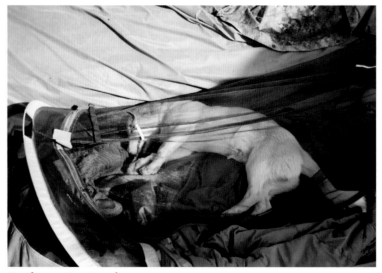

Fred napping in a bug net. *(Courtesy of Craig Grossi)*

Craig holding Fred in Afghanistan. *(Courtesy of Dave Moran)*

Fred flying home. *(Courtesy of Sergio Giacchetti)*

Craig and Fred on the road. *(Courtesy of Nora Parkington)*

Getting ready to hit the road. *(Courtesy of Michael Erhardt)*

Craig and Fred in front of the Grand Canyon. *(Courtesy of Josh Tuohy)*

Beach camping in Coos Bay, Oregon. *(Courtesy of Josh Tuohy)*

Fred in Maine with Ruby. *(Courtesy of Craig Grossi)*

Fred and Nora. *(Courtesy of Craig Grossi)*

The command decided our patrol would return back to the other compound that night, rejoining the rest of the company. Our ammunition supply was low and our position was too vulnerable.

We waited for nightfall, enduring the heat and the disquiet. A few hours after sunset, finally, it was time to step off. We put our game faces on, but after a day like that, you realize how fragile everything is. Even though we weren't safe in the compound, it still felt more secure than the exposure and unknown of the Green Zone. None of us was looking forward to patrolling back through Taliban territory. Before we slipped between the tall, whispering cornstalks of the first field, I turned to Justin and Ysa and bumped my fist into theirs. "I love you guys," I whispered, then pushed my way into the sea of corn.

On the other side of the cornfield, we encountered another flooded field. It was worse now. The soil was so saturated, water pooled on top of the mud, reflecting glassy, glimmering streaks of moonlight. We trudged into the cold, sucking soil, sinking hip-deep. Midway through the first field, one of the marines sunk into it up to his chest, and Ysa and I pulled him out, leaving his boots behind.

Slowly, we worked our way through the next flooded field, and then the next. It became clear this was part of the Taliban's plan. They knew we cut through fields; they knew where we needed to go. If we were slow, stuck, and vulnerable, they could unload on us. And halfway through our retreat, they did. A *pop-pop-pop* sputtered through the mud near the patrol. Thankfully, though, it was just one guy taking inaccurate shots from far away. Our sniper went to the back of the patrol and lay in the mud, trying to get a shot at him.

To say we were miserable would be an understatement. We were mentally and physically exhausted. The mud was relentless, and the erratic pop shots were almost enough to make you come unhinged. What should have taken us a couple of hours was taking all night.

With less than an hour before sunrise, we came upon a final canal. It was the one nearest to our compound—the first one we always crossed when we left the desert and ventured into the Green Zone. We called it the "Mini Helmand" because of its size; it was wide and deep, one of the only ones that had a current to it instead of dead, still water. Once we got through it, our compound wasn't far off. We were almost home.

But something was wrong. As we approached the canal, I could hear it. When we'd crossed it the night before, the water had been up to our hips. Now, though, the current was raging, and it looked twice as deep.

When the young marine serving as point man attempted to cross the canal, he was almost overcome by the current. We were all exhausted, carrying heavy gear and wearing armor. If you lost your footing in water like that, you'd get pulled under, swept away.

A few other guys headed downstream to try and find a less treacherous place to ford the mini-river but came up short. Our patrol had been stopped for a while now in the open field. We were running out of time.

Not far off, we saw an archway of packed mud, about shoulder width wide. A bridge.

What if we took the easy route? We discussed it. It was too obvious: the Taliban knew where we were headed; they knew the muddy fields would delay us; they knew we'd end up here. A bottleneck. It was too risky. But it was also risky—incredibly risky—to be caught out in the open when the sun rose. We'd be sitting ducks. The bridge was tempting.

The point man volunteered to check the bridge with a mine-sweeper. If no IED was found, we'd be out of here. The problem was, we never wholly trusted minesweepers. They only detected metal, and plenty of IEDs were mostly wood and plastic. Only the switching mechanism needed to be metal—sometimes it was something as simple as an aluminum foil gum wrapper. The sweeper could miss it altogether.

Fifteen, twenty minutes had passed. Too long. We were still getting shot at; occasionally a round buzzed by, slapping the swollen earth. The sun would rise soon.

Justin pulled Ysa aside. "I can't let that kid go up there with that sweeper. We'll be sending him to die," he said.

Then Justin volunteered to go. "Let me get up there," he said. "If there's an IED, I'll find it."

Carefully, Justin approached the bridge, sweeping the metal detector from right to left in front of him, just like you'd look for coins on the beach. Ysa followed behind, maybe ten feet back, so he could talk with Justin while he worked. EOD technicians always work in teams. Our patrol fanned out in the field around them, and I stood back, next to my ruck, watching in the distance.

When he reached the foot of the bridge, Justin placed the minesweeper behind him. He lowered himself onto his hands and knees. The only way to clear the bridge was through a manual, painstaking process. Justin pulled out a knife and methodically began pressing the tip of it into the dirt in front of him, then slowly lifting it. He progressed forward, carefully digging and lifting, digging and lifting. He was searching for wires. If he lifted the knife and pulled up wires attached to an IED, he'd determine the best way to separate the pressure plate from the jug of explosive. Or, since we wouldn't have much time, we could simply rule out the bridge and be forced to figure out a way through the canal. Justin was expert at clearing IEDs. He'd done it more than a hundred times on his last deployment in Iraq.

We waited in the field. I could just make out Justin working his way across the bridge, his hands moving steadily under the red glow of his headlamp while Ysa stood behind him.

About a quarter of the way over the bridge, Justin's knife caught something. Slowly, he lifted it, drawing two wires from the dirt. He'd found it.

Cautiously, Justin got to his feet on the narrow mud bridge. He looked back at Ysa, signaling to confirm what he'd found. In the same moment, incomprehensibly, I heard a loud, deep blast. The bridge erupted in a black cloud of dirt and mud.

I felt the blast in my body like a thud to the chest. My ears rang. Ysa was knocked backward.

I stood, mind racing. Sometimes, IEDs didn't completely detonate. Sometimes, they were just duds. Sometimes, no one got hurt. Sometimes, everything was okay.

Then I heard Justin scream. I'll never forget the sound. He wasn't screaming in pain. It was a cry of disappointment. It was as though he was apologizing—to us, to himself, to his family.

I started running.

Ysa got to Justin first, followed by Doc Jones.

At the site of the explosion, an IED blast crushes your body. The pressure destroys tissue. Justin's right leg was gone from the hip down. His left leg was badly mangled from foot to thigh.

Conscious but disoriented, he began trying to say he'd found the IED, that we shouldn't take the bridge.

"Is everyone else okay?" Justin asked Ysa.

"Yes. We're okay. We got you, buddy," Ysa said.

Justin had been thrown into the bank of a smaller canal that fed into the one we needed to cross.

When I got there, Ysa and Doc Jones had already applied a tourniquet to each of Justin's legs. He was on a litter. Doc Jones ran an IV and handed me the bag. Someone was on the radio. I knew we didn't have much time.

We kept talking to him. "Hang in there," we said. "Justin, you're the man. Don't worry. Just breathe."

Justin's breathing was labored; his blood pressure began to drop. Doc placed a mouthpiece over his lips with a tube attached to it. Ysa took the IV bag from my hands, and just like I had with Sean, I leaned over and breathed air into Justin's lungs. Every few seconds, I exhaled, and Justin's chest rose. The guys were all there. We continued to talk to him. He began to lose consciousness. It was as though he was falling asleep.

Overhead, we heard an eerie *whoop-whoop-whoop* sound. Canisters of infrared illumination tumbled through the air like strange, slow fireworks. They'd been fired from the artillery battery on the Kajaki Dam to provide light so the helicopter pilots could safely land.

We heard Tricky on the horizon. It's a special medevac for amputees. The bird is a Chinook, the kind with two rotors—essentially a flying ER. I remember hearing the accents of the British crew over the radio. As the helicopter came down, we lifted Justin and ran through the mud toward its open hatch. I held the litter in my right hand while carrying Justin's flak vest in my left. A part of my brain was on autopilot, from training; I'd picked up his vest because I knew you were never supposed to fly without it.

We ran Justin up the ramp and laid him down among a team of trauma nurses and surgeons, who got to work immediately. I dropped Justin's armor and stood there, unable to move. My face and hands were covered in blood and mud. I reached one hand out to my friend and touched his chest. Then I backed away.

When the Chinook took off, we took cover from the rotor wash. Under the deafening sound, I lay facedown in the mud and screamed into the cold, wet earth until my throat hurt. My head throbbed. Nothing made sense. Part of me knew Justin was gone, but another part of me couldn't comprehend it.

Somehow, I got up. Ysa was collecting Justin's stuff at the blast site, trying to do a quick postblast investigation. He picked up pieces of Justin's rifle, which had been blown to bits, and we hooked Justin's ruck to mine so I could carry it back. By now the sun was almost up. The QRF—quick reaction force—had arrived from our compound. They put ladders into the water so we could cross the canal. We made our way back.

CRAIG & FRED   219

Ysa and I went into our little room. We started going through Justin's stuff, getting it organized. The front of Ysa's uniform was drenched in his friend's blood.

Without looking up, Ysa said quietly, "Justin didn't make it." He'd heard it over the radio.

"I know," I said quietly. "I'm so sorry, man."

We didn't talk much that day. I think we all felt numb. The room was pretty dark and stayed cool during the day. We stayed in there and watched *Dumb and Dumber* and *Step Brothers* on my laptop between sleep. At some point, Ysa called home to his wife.

Later, there was a patrol debrief meeting in the compound with everybody. I showed up. The RECON captain told the team that Justin hadn't made it. There was bad news about Sean, too. He was alive but "expectant"—meaning he was expected to pass away. He was being flown to Germany, where his parents could come and say good-bye. He was gone.

A few nights later, we extracted. Back at Leatherneck, for twenty-four hours, I didn't do anything. Mac and Sergio and the rest of the guys gave me space. I showered, then lay in bed, trying to sleep. After that, I dove back into work. The detention facility was pretty full; there were plenty of detainees to inter-rogate and process. The days were long. I'd spend hours in the interrogation booth, then hours afterward doing paperwork. I kept busy. I kept moving.

The day of Justin's memorial service on Leatherneck, I couldn't bring myself to go. Instead, I purposely scheduled an interrogation. I was still too angry. I replayed the events of the whole mission over in my head, searching for mistakes. I went through all the *what-ifs,* over and over. What if I'd gotten more involved in planning the patrol? I could have looked at the compound the team planned to take and realized there wasn't enough standoff. What if I'd said something different at the canal? Maybe I could have convinced the point man or Justin that the bridge wasn't an option.

What if. What if. What if.

CHAPTER 15

Disservice

As we drove away from Portland and headed toward our last big destination of the trip, Seattle, we didn't take the scenic route. I pulled the Land Cruiser onto the highway and pressed my foot against the accelerator, pushing the truck toward her top speed of fifty-five miles per hour. It was midmorning, midweek; the roads were quiet and the sky was gray. Fred, after nearly eight weeks on the road, knew the drill by now. He curled up on his blankets in the backseat, let out a sigh, and closed his eyes, resting up for wherever we were taking him next. But we weren't headed toward a lake or a canyon or a trailhead or a campsite. We were taking Josh to the hospital.

The issue wasn't with his prosthetic this time; it was his good leg that was giving him problems. He thought it might be a blood clot, which scared the shit out of me. In Seattle, we planned to stay with a friend of Josh's from the army, Matt, and go to the VA hospital in town.

When we were back in Portland, as we'd walked around the city, I'd noticed Josh's gait was different. He was leaning into his prosthetic more than usual, favoring his left leg and limping a little. When Josh said he was in pain, it became clear that he'd been uncomfortable for a while and had been keeping it to himself, maybe not wanting to deal with it or feel like he was holding us back. I thought about all the demanding hiking we'd done in Los Padres, the redwoods, and Crater Lake, wondering if we'd pushed it too far.

When we pulled up to his apartment, Matt met us outside. He looked like he could have been Josh's brother. The two of them were both tall and thin, with big smiles and similar mannerisms. They each tilted their heads in the same inquisitive way when they listened to someone talk, and Matt shared Josh's knack for blunt sarcasm. Matt had been one of the medics in Josh's unit. Now, he was in the army reserve and had a civilian job as an X-ray tech at a local hospital.

"So, you've been on the road with a jarhead this long and you haven't gotten lost?" Matt said jokingly to Josh after he introduced me.

"No, but we had to stop a lot so this guy could call his mommy and ask if he could stay out a little longer," I teased.

Once the jokes and introductions were over, I knew I had to let Matt know what was going on.

"We should get Josh to the hospital, though," I said. "His leg is getting worse."

I wanted to be the one to say it—to take the pressure off Josh.

We dropped off our gear with Matt, then Josh and I got right back in the truck. The VA hospital was just fifteen minutes away, but on the short drive over, neither of us spoke. I knew Josh's biggest fear was that someday he'd have to have his good leg amputated. What if all the surgeries and all the physical therapy weren't enough to repair the badly damaged tissue?

He'd shown me the scars on his leg where shrapnel had sliced through muscle, where surgeons had worked to make repairs. I'd known other combat vets—and certainly Josh had, too— who eventually lost a limb that could never be saved.

Yet, all summer, I'd made it a point to treat Josh the same way I would have treated any of my other buddies. I didn't want him to feel that I doubted what he was capable of or that I was babying him because of his prosthetic. If we were on a trail and he needed to rest, I'd sit with him and wait. I didn't look at him and ask, "Are you okay?" with pity or worry. I knew he wanted to push himself, and I wanted to help him do that, not to get in the way.

Now that something was clearly wrong, it was hard to find the right words. I didn't know what to say to my friend who had been through so much just to be able to walk. Josh had challenged himself more than I could even imagine throughout his recovery, and especially on our trip. He'd accomplished so much, and he'd been a good friend to me, listening to me tell Fred's story over and over again to so many of the people we met without ever complaining, waiting for me when I wanted to mountain-bike, and just putting up with me for two months straight.

When we got to the VA, I pulled Josh in for a quick hug.

"Hey, man—at least you know your way around a VA hospital. You should be able to get seen pretty quick," I said. Josh knew I was being sarcastic—no appointment at the VA could ever be described as "quick."

"Yeah, bro. I'll be in and out," Josh said, not looking at me. "Go have fun with Matt—he's a great guy." He rubbed Fred's head and let the dog lick his face before turning and hopping out of the truck.

Fred and I watched as Josh limped down the breezeway and through the lobby doors. I shifted the truck into drive and headed back to Matt's, where we'd wait to get an update from Josh. On the drive, Fred didn't climb into Josh's seat, as he usually would have. Instead, he stayed in the back with his head down, as if he knew something wasn't right. In the past two months, our tight little group had rarely ever separated from one another. I let out a sigh and glanced back at Fred in the backseat. I wanted to feel optimistic, but I couldn't help the sinking feeling that this was where Josh's trip ended.

When you get home from combat, people have a way of talking to you like they're waiting for you to implode. It's kind of like the way your mom talks to you when you're sick. There's a different tone of voice—everything is a higher pitch. A simple "How are you doing?" feels loaded. When I first got home from Afghanistan, I resented that. So when it came to talking about Sangin with family and friends, I'm pretty sure I gave off a continuous *I don't want to talk about it* vibe. I didn't want people to think something was wrong with me, and talking about it only opened the door for that possibility. So it was a long time before I ever told anyone about what happened to Sean or Justin.

One day, after I'd been home for over a year, Ysa called. He and another EOD technician, Ed, a guy who had known Justin, along with one of the RECON guys, Patrick, were heading to D.C. for a weekend course at Quantico, a base in Virginia. Ysa was still in the marines, and we talked every so often, but he spent most of his off-duty time, understandably, with his wife and kids. I was pumped that the guys were coming to my city, and I invited all three of them to stay with me. In my tiny studio apartment, the guys laid out sleeping mats and crammed in. All weekend, we partied like fraternity brothers. It felt good to be around guys who had seen combat, who had been to Sangin and had known Justin—guys who got it.

That Saturday, I planned a big night at my favorite bar, the Pug, and invited my high school buddies. "You need to come meet my guys from Afghanistan," I told them. I was looking forward to having my best friends all in one place.

That night, I had everyone drinking whiskey and Stroh's, that beer Justin and I joked about in Afghanistan. I always drank it at the Pug in his honor. Irish punk music played in the background as Tony and Chaz, my favorite bartenders, dished out shots and beer. It was crowded, but most of the people were locals and regulars I recognized. I felt at home, and we were having a blast.

Then, at one point, I walked up to a conversation between Ysa and my high school friend Brian. As I approached, I realized Ysa was telling the story of the night Justin was killed. I stiffened up. He was describing the mud bridge and the IED. Ysa pointed to me, saying how I'd helped perform first aid on Justin before the Chinook arrived.

I felt a cool rush of anxiety sweep through me. I thought about that night all the time. Every time it was quiet—late at night in bed, as I was trying to sleep—my mind went to Afghanistan. I'd lie there restless and half-awake, and the visions from Sangin would come. They felt like dream-memories—part real, part imagined. Sometimes I saw myself sitting around a fire in the compound with the guys. Other times, I stood at a murder hole looking through the scope of my rifle. In the crosshairs, a figure carrying an AK-47 would appear. I'd pull the trigger and the figure would drop, but then I'd spot another one and another until I'd wake up. And other times—many, many times—my mind went back to the night on the bridge with Justin. I relived the last moments by the canal. I retraced each word that passed our lips before Justin decided to clear the bridge. *Why didn't you stop him?* I'd ask myself, again and again.

At the bar, Ysa saw the look on my face and began to realize what was going on. The friends I'd been hanging out with all this time—the people I'd known practically all my life—didn't have a clue about that night. I'd told them stories from Afghanistan, about Fred, of course, and Leatherneck and the RECON marines, but I'd never talked about Justin or Sean. I shot Ysa a look, as if to say, "Please, dude, shut up." He wrapped up his story, then the two of us found a spot at the bar.

"Let's do a shot for Justin," I said. Now that Ysa had brought it up, my mind was awash with memories. Chaz poured three shots of Jameson: one for me, one for Ysa, and one for Justin. We took ours and left the third sitting on the bar.

My eyes fell on the untouched glass of Justin's whiskey, then to Ysa's wrist, where I'd noticed he wore a memorial bracelet. It was a black metal wristband with Justin's name, title, and KIA date and location. It was common for guys to wear them in remembrance of friends they'd lost.

Ysa pulled off the bracelet. "This is yours, man," he said, putting it on my wrist. "I want you to have it."

I felt a burn rise up in my throat and eyes, and I couldn't choke back the tears. The gift of the bracelet was a small and simple act, but, in that moment, it meant everything to me. Right there in the bar, I broke down completely, as if a year's worth of repressed emotion were flooding out. I cried hard, my head in my hands. Ysa put his arms around me and we hugged. For the next ten minutes, I tried to pull it together, but I couldn't. Ed, Patrick, and Brian all came over to see what was going on. They tried to console me, gathering around me with their arms locked around my back, but there was no way for me to compose myself. All I could think about was Justin. Eventually, Ysa and the guys got me out of the bar and took me home.

The next morning, I woke up in bed and looked down at the guys lying on their mats on the floor. At my feet, Fred looked up at me, and slowly Ysa, Patrick, and Ed woke up, too. Right away, I put a smile on my face and started talking about what we were going to have for breakfast. I tried to brush off what had happened the night before. But I could tell the guys were worried about me. For Ysa, Pat, and Ed, things were different. They were all still on active duty, so they were around each other and around other marines all the time, working, relaxing, shooting the shit, and talking about stuff—the good and the bad. I think they realized that for me, since I'd gotten out of the marines, it was different. I had come home to civilian life and just kept going.

"You can't keep that stuff inside, man," Ysa said. "You gotta talk about it. You gotta find an outlet."

It was the first time I remember anyone really calling me out on the way I was coping—or not coping—after coming home. And I respected the way Ysa talked to me. He wasn't coddling me; he wasn't looking at me like I was broken. He simply told me I was wrong, in a way only a fellow marine could. It was just factual—almost as if I'd been slacking off on working out and had gotten out of shape, and he wanted me to get it together. "You're only doing a disservice to yourself," Ysa said. It was my duty to take care of it—to take care of myself.

"If you're not dealing and talking, you're taking yourself out of the fight. It's not gonna end well," Ysa said.

I knew he was right.

Back in Seattle, Matt and I waited for an update from Josh, who'd been at the VA hospital for a few hours.

"You know, if it is a blood clot, it's a good thing you stopped in Portland," Matt said. Portland hadn't been a stop Josh and I planned to make. After Josh's moment of cliff-jumping fame in Crater Lake, a couple and their three grown kids approached him and struck up a conversation. They'd invited us to use their campsite in Bend, where we were already planning to go, and afterward, their oldest daughter, Heather, insisted we see Portland. "You can use my apartment and I'll stay with my boyfriend. It's right in the Pearl District, so you'd have a great time," she offered, insisting we shouldn't miss the city. We'd planned to make the six-hour drive from our camping spot in Bend up to Seattle but ended up taking a detour at Heather's urging.

"What do you mean it's good we stopped in Portland?" I asked Matt. The two of us were sitting at the dog park watching Fred and Matt's white Labrador, Lucy, chase each other.

"Clots usually get worse during periods of rest, when someone sits still for an extended period of time. If you had driven all the way up to Seattle from Bend, one of the clots could have traveled up to Josh's brain or his heart. That could have killed him," Matt said with the matter-of-fact tone unique to medical professionals.

"Holy shit," I said, trying to grapple with how bad things could have been.

I thought back on the trip and considered the close calls we'd had, from the Land Cruiser nearly sinking in the Mississippi mud to Josh's prosthetic giving out in the middle of the redwoods. We'd come so far and seen so much, managing to get by with only a few mishaps. Still, those mishaps could have been really serious had things gone only slightly differently. Maybe this latest close call was our final warning.

As the sun began to set, I decided to get Fred settled in at Matt's and head back to the hospital. The last text I'd received from Josh said he was still waiting to see the doctor. I figured I'd go wait in the lobby. I didn't want him to feel alone.

Under the fluorescent lights of the VA lobby, I made a crappy cup of coffee from a vending machine and took a seat in a stiff plastic chair. In front of me was a big coffee table with magazines spread across it—*VFW, Military Spouse, Highlights.* A few elderly veterans wearing Vietnam vet ball caps sat quietly in wheelchairs or with walkers. The group appeared to be waiting for a bus back to their assisted-living facility. I didn't speak to any of them, but I always felt bad thinking about the way veterans of that era were treated when they came home. Many of them had been drafted into the conflict and saw combat that left them physically and mentally scarred. The society they'd returned to was a far cry from our current "Thank you for your service" spirit. Plus, the VA and all the other resources weren't as robust then as they are today. It was something I tried to remind myself of any time I found myself complaining about the VA.

A text came in from Josh: "Blood clots. They wrote me a prescription. I'll be out in 10."

I was relieved they weren't making him stay in the hospital, but I knew we weren't out of the woods. About twenty minutes later, Josh came through the doors carrying a shopping bag of meds. He was still limping a little bit, but there he was, smiling and on his feet.

"Hey, man, you didn't have to wait for me," he said.

"Well, I really wanted to get a look at the lobby of the Seattle VA. It was right up there on my must-see list with the Grand Canyon and the redwoods," I joked as we walked out. The bus was loading the last wheelchaired veteran as we got into the Land Cruiser.

"I never thought I'd be so happy to see the inside of this beauty," Josh said as he clipped his seat belt. He explained how he'd been prescribed a blood thinner that he'd need to inject into his stomach twice a day, along with some pain meds.

"The doctor told me to take it easy, but she didn't say anything about not traveling," he said.

I paused a moment, genuinely surprised that he didn't seem to be considering packing it in and catching the next flight home. From what Josh was saying, it sounded like the medication wasn't really a "fix"—just enough to make him comfortable till he got back to his regular doctor in D.C. But I didn't say anything.

"If you wanna keep going, it's your call. I just don't want you to drop dead on me. That would really kill the trip," I joked.

"I always thought my time would come in the passenger seat of a Land Cruiser—I just didn't think it'd be this soon," he replied with a smile.

A few days later, at a bar in Minneapolis, we had our first big fight of the trip. We were staying with Josh's high school friend Alex, who took us to a Twins game. Afterward, we went to a bar by the stadium for oversize soft pretzels and a few beers. All night, I'd noticed Josh had been favoring his leg, leaning into the prosthetic. I was concerned about him, especially because the rest of the trip would be all driving. I only had enough money for gas and food, and I planned on going straight through from Minneapolis to D.C.

"Hey, man. You feeling okay? How's your leg?" I said, trying to keep it casual.

"Yeah—I'm fine, man. Why?" Josh said.

"You just looked a little uncomfortable while we were walking around tonight. I realized I hadn't really asked you about your leg in a while," I said.

The truth was, things had been tense between us since Seattle. After saying good-bye to Matt, we drove ten long hours to Bozeman, Montana. We camped overnight and I went for one last long mountain bike ride, then it was onward to North Dakota, where we camped under the most brilliant stars we'd ever seen. Then we'd made our way to Minneapolis, Josh's hometown. Nothing had happened, but the whole time, I could feel a strain between us that wasn't there before.

Even though I wasn't saying it, I was annoyed because I thought Josh was putting his health at risk. We both knew he'd done more on this trip on one leg than we ever thought possible. It was incredible. Now why didn't he know when to call it quits? He should have flown home from Seattle and seen his doctor back home, I thought. I wanted Josh to understand the difference between doing something worthwhile to challenge himself and doing something dangerous just for the sake of doing it. Instead of acknowledging the reality of his pain, he was ignoring it. To me, it was obvious. What was much harder for me to see was how the things I was saying to Josh applied directly to me, too.

"Look. Why don't you just say it? You think I should fly home. I can tell you've been thinking it," Josh said.

"Shouldn't you listen to the doctors in Seattle? Didn't they say riding in the car could be bad for the clots? That's pretty much all we're gonna do between here and D.C.," I said.

"If you want me off the trip, just say it," he said, clearly upset.

We'd had a few beers, and after all this time on the road together, we were on each other's nerves. It was easy for the conversation to escalate. Alex came back from the restroom and saw we were in some sort of discussion. She let us be, walking over to the bar with her friends.

"I want you to make that decision. I want you to take a look at your situation and deal with it instead of sweeping it under the rug and making it someone else's problem," I said sharply. "You've seen this summer what you're capable of. How far you can push yourself mentally and physically. Now you need to accept your limitations."

The next morning, I drove Josh to the airport. Our argument at the bar hadn't gone anywhere productive, and when we got back to Alex's apartment, I went to bed and Josh booked a flight. Now we were in the truck again, and it was quiet.

We got out at the departures terminal and stood on the pavement at the back of the Land Cruiser. Cars went by and people hurried through revolving doors. I reached for Josh's duffel bag and handed it to him. We looked at each other, managed smiles, and even hugged.

"Thanks, man," Josh said earnestly. "I had a great time." He gave Fred a kiss on the head.

"I couldn't have done it without you, man. I'm really glad you came," I told him. It was true.

In the front seat, Fred didn't whimper or complain. He seemed to understand that it was Josh's time to leave our little pack. I shifted the Land Cruiser into gear and pointed us in the direction of home.

CHAPTER 16

Homecoming

After my last mission in Afghanistan, during the final days of my deployment, my buddy PJ and I sat in our barracks on Leatherneck and drank. We'd had a bottle of Johnnie Walker Red Label stashed away since we'd first arrived in-country. For seven months, it waited for us.

"Before we go home—when we know we're done with field operations—we're gonna drink this whole thing, me and you," I'd said to PJ. That felt like a long time ago now.

We brought Coke back from the chow hall and sat across from each other on our bunks, our packed bags around us, passing the bottle back and forth. We hadn't had a lick of alcohol in seven months and we were each down a good fifteen pounds, so it didn't take much for the booze to do its thing.

PJ and I had trained in intelligence together before coming over on the same deployment. We'd been roommates, too. We were close. Back at Pendleton, when we were preparing to deploy, our command informed us there would be only two positions for intel collectors out in the field, both up at the infantry-held base at the Kajaki Dam. The rest of us should expect to spend our deployment on Camp Leatherneck. We knew the fighting in Kajaki was bad, that the marines there had suffered a lot of casualties, but the thought of spending our deployment sitting at a desk was devastating. PJ and I both wanted that placement in the field doing what we'd trained to do.

Later, our commander, Gomez, pulled me and PJ aside. He knew how close we were. "PJ, you're going to Kajaki," he said. "Craig, you'll be on Camp Leatherneck. I can't have you two in one place; I need one of you here." We all knew PJ and I made the best team, but he couldn't send two close friends out into that environment. If something happened to one of us out there, it'd compromise the other's ability to continue the mission.

I was crushed. Little did we know at the time what lay ahead for me.

Back in the barracks, PJ and I started swapping stories about what we'd seen and done in our time apart. Our deployments turned out to be relatively similar. PJ had seen some serious combat in Kajaki. The Taliban wanted to regain control of the dam, so they were relentless. And since it was a known coalition base, the whole surrounding area was heavily laced with IEDs. PJ had seen guys evaporate in front of him. One moment your buddy was there, the next moment he was gone.

There aren't many words for things like that. He knew, and I knew, what it was like, and that was enough.

After Sean and Justin died, I went on one last, long mission. Instead of inserting by helicopter, we drove MRAPs and M-ATVs out into the desert. We took a compound—one big enough that we could drive the vehicles into it—that Ysa and Bobby, Justin's replacement, cleared. It got turned into a patrol base: PB Alcatraz. Eventually, tents, barracks, and showers would be flown in. The coalition would use it to secure the area, including the stretch of 611 leading toward the dam.

On that mission, a lot of things happened in Sangin that I thought I'd never see. After a few weeks of harsh fighting, we started to see villagers moving about during the day. Kids were running around, chasing each other, playing in the sand. A local market—a little mud-walled structure by the side of the 611—reopened. We started leaving the compound during the day, meeting and talking with more villagers than we ever had before. Ysa and I would go to the little market and buy produce—cucumbers, apples, figs, pears—almost like we were grocery shopping back home. My rifle became a burden—as if it were a hassle to carry it. For a while, things in Sangin were relatively peaceful. It felt like a completely different place.

Then we started to see what we called "combat tourists" arrive on our base: majors, colonels, and other high-ranking leadership. They'd fly in from Leatherneck and demand to go out on "presence patrols," which basically meant taking a walk through Taliban town in the middle of the day like a bunch of tourists. These patrols were dangerous because they didn't serve any purpose. There wasn't a group of villagers we were hoping to talk with, and the routes were loosely planned. It was as if they wanted to be able to say they'd patrolled in Sangin without actually having to spend any real time there. It was dangerous, and I didn't see the tactical benefit. To me, it was a sign the bureaucratic war machine had caught up with us. I was ready to come home.

Still, I didn't feel good about getting out of there when other guys had to stay. After Justin died, Ysa and I got really close, along with Bobby, Justin's replacement. Bobby had joined us after recovering from a gunshot wound to his left bicep; he was a welcome addition to our crew of misfits. When I left, Ysa and Bobby still had another four months on their deployment. I felt like I was abandoning them, and I couldn't shake the feeling that one day I'd wake up to a call with news that something had happened to one of them.

When PJ and I finished the bottle, I slept better than I had in a long while. A few days later, I'd be on a plane to Camp Pendleton, where I would turn in my gear and get processed out of First Intelligence Battalion. Then, at last, it'd be home to Virginia and to Fred, who'd been waiting for more than three months for me to come home.

It was strange to be on a commercial jet in civilian clothes, but I felt good. I liked going unrecognized, just a regular guy on a plane. Instead of cammies, I wore my blue Capitals cap, jeans, and a sweatshirt. I watched movies on my iPad. I didn't feel particularly emotional. I was excited to see Fred, excited to get back and move on.

When we touched down at Reagan, I walked through the terminal and there they were: my mom, dad, stepmom, stepdad, my sister and her family, my then-girlfriend, and a bunch of high school buddies. They had a huge banner. WELCOME HOME CRAIG! it read in big block letters. They wore homemade T-shirts with my face on them and waved little American flags.

I fixed a big grin on my face and walked toward them. It wasn't a phony smile; I was glad to see them—surprised, actually. I didn't know they were all going to be there, especially with the sign and shirts. But before I knew what I was thinking, just like that, my mind went to Sean and Justin. Their families weren't going to get to have this moment. The thought sent a wave of rage and regret through my body. I felt sick.

I hadn't told anyone too much about my deployment. When I got injured, I didn't want to freak out my family. I almost didn't call at all. Then a couple of guys at Leatherneck told me that sometimes, in reports that got sent back home, names from the WIA list could accidentally get put onto the KIA list. I didn't want to think about what it'd do to my mom and dad if somehow they were falsely notified that I had been killed. So I called them both and carefully delivered a watered-down version of the rocket explosion that almost blew me to pieces.

Still, no one knew much, which was fine before, when I was over there. Now that I was standing in front of everyone, it felt different. I didn't know what my friends had heard—if they thought I was fucked up in the head now. I worried that everyone would think I was a different person, that my injury and my time in Afghanistan had changed who I was.

I put myself on cruise control, going numb to the noise of my emotions. I kept that smile going and took turns hugging and thanking everyone. My mom, who wore my high school ice hockey jersey, was sobbing as she pulled me in for a long, tight embrace. Then I hugged my dad, and over his shoulder caught sight of Sarah, who was crying, too. She was holding my little niece Sam, who was born just before I deployed and was now almost a year old.

My family took me to a seafood place near the airport. We got seated at a big long table in the middle of the restaurant. It was crowded and noisy, and I remember looking around, thinking, *Where are the exits?* And then, *Where are Ysa and Bobby?* People kept walking behind me; I watched everyone who went by, trying to listen to anything they might say.

I didn't have much of an appetite, but I ordered the surf and turf. Everything was drenched in butter, and I was coming off months of bland cafeteria food and MREs. I ate a few bites and pushed the rest of it around on my plate.

No one really knew how to ask me questions or what to say. I didn't blame them. Someone eventually asked something about what it was like over there, but it was easy to deflect. "It was hot," I said with a grin.

Thankfully, there was one thing all of us were happy to talk about, and that was Fred. Sarah jumped in and started telling stories about him. On the weekends, she'd gone to my dad's to give him and my stepmom a break from taking care of Fred. She'd take Fred on walks and play with him. She laughed as she told me how Fred didn't understand fetch. He would bring back a ball, but then he'd never drop it. Instead, he wanted her to try to get it from him or play tug-of-war.

A few times, she talked about watching Fred sit out on the front lawn, nose up in the air, sniffing and looking into the distance. It made her cry, she said, realizing that Fred may have been wondering where I was.

"I really think he was waiting for you," she said.

My dad still lived in the house we grew up in, and my bedroom was still the same as it had been since childhood: same bed, same furniture, some clothes in the closet. Once, Sarah had been sitting on the couch with Fred, watching TV, when she realized he'd snuck away. She called out his name but didn't hear anything. After searching the house, she finally found him. He was upstairs in my bedroom, on my bed, his head resting on my pillow.

Back in Afghanistan, my mind often wandered to Fred. I wondered what he was doing, what mischief he was getting into. I hoped he'd remember me. I hoped that I'd make it back to see him.

When dinner finally ended, we headed back to my dad's house. On the way home, he explained how he'd turned the basement into Fred's little lair. Apparently Fred loved the carpeting down there—better traction for running and playing. When we arrived at the house, I raced straight to the basement. My dad had been trying to crate-train Fred, so he was in this big metal crate, surrounded by pillows. As I came down the steps, the first thing I heard was his tail slapping against the metal. "Hey, buddy!" I called to him, and his tail stopped wagging. He got a good look at my face, and I swear he did a double take. There was a moment's pause as he drew in a gasp of air, then he let out a long, slow howl, like he couldn't believe it was me.

When I reached the bottom of the stairs, I opened the gate, and Fred went nuts. He was all over me, jumping and nipping and flipping around. He ran between my legs, rubbing against my shins with his butt while he continued to let out excited howl-whines. I lay right down on the floor and let him jump on my chest and lick my face.

He looked like a new dog. His fur was soft and fluffy, each strand set free from the weight of dust. He wore a green camouflage collar with FRED stitched on the side in big brown letters. He looked like he'd gained a little weight, too.

"Damn, buddy! You're domesticated now," I laughed, grabbing a rope toy so we could play.

I couldn't believe I was here with Fred in my childhood home. The last time I'd seen him, he'd been in a kennel getting loaded onto a cargo jet. But something about this setting felt natural, too. Fred seemed comfortable, as if he'd always been there, as if we had always been together.

Even though it was cold and dark outside, I decided to take Fred for a walk. My family was buzzing with excitement and I just wanted a moment of quiet. I grabbed the leash my dad had bought, and the two of us headed out the door. We walked down a little dirt path that wound through the neighborhood. It was the same path I used to walk Irene and the other neighborhood dogs on when I was a kid, longing for a dog of my own.

I was impressed by how well Fred did on the leash. He trotted alongside me, looking up every few steps as if to make sure it was really me. I smiled down at him, and we walked together in the moonlight.

In the following days, I got a full Fred report from my dad. It was funny to me that my dad—who had never wanted us to have a dog as kids because he knew he'd end up doing all the work—had taken care of Fred all this time. But it actually seemed like he'd enjoyed it. He told me Fred had been really well behaved from the start. He ate anything you gave him and slept anywhere soft. Even though Fred had never lived in a house before, he'd somehow understood potty training immediately, maybe since he had only ever done his business outside. Fred was smart, though. My dad told me how Fred quickly figured out that, on walks, as soon as he went to the bathroom, the walk was over. So he began holding it, forcing my dad to go on longer and longer odysseys before he'd finally go.

One thing that scared him was curbside sewer drains. Something about the dark hole in the ground totally unnerved him. My dad would have to avoid drains entirely; otherwise, Fred would freeze up. A few times, my dad even picked up Fred and carried him past one because he wouldn't budge.

Another thing Fred didn't care for was being groomed. Since his fur was pretty long, my dad figured it would be a good idea to take Fred to the groomer. So he dropped the dog off one day and a couple of hours later returned to pick him up. Neither Fred nor the groomer looked very happy. "He really barks loudly," the groomer said with a frown. Apparently Fred had had a lot to say about his new haircut.

In general, Fred seemed happiest outside. He loved sitting out on the front lawn, just taking in the smells and rolling around in the grass. He also loved the snow. The first time he saw it, he was amazed. He stuck his long snout into it, using it as a plow to push the cold white stuff around.

My dad warned me that Fred was fascinated by wood, so much so that he'd chewed up some furniture in the house. He was a bit impatient, too. One morning, my dad hurried to drink his coffee before taking Fred out for his morning walk. Apparently, Dad wasn't fast enough. Tired of waiting, Fred sunk his front fangs into the molding around the door and popped off the entire frame in one tug.

While I was still on my deployment, my dad had been pretty protective of Fred. If anything had happened to the dog before I got home, my dad wouldn't have been able to live with himself. So, aside from a few trips to the vet for vaccines and to get neutered, Fred mostly spent his time inside or on leashed walks.

Now that I was home, I couldn't wait to take Fred on adventures and start our new life together. I quickly realized, though, that there would be a learning curve for both of us. We were starting over, in a different city, in a different country, and had to get to know each other again.

That summer, even with the humidity, Fred still had a lot of energy. He always wanted to be outside, and nothing seemed to tire him out. As he'd done at my dad's house, he chewed around the base of my apartment door and even along the windowsills—anything that looked like an exit. Sometimes he'd start gnawing on the doorframe right in front of me, right after we came in from a long walk. "Fred!" I'd shout, completely exasperated.

We started spending a lot of time at the dog park. At first, Fred didn't really understand how to play with other dogs. He had met other dogs before but hadn't really been socialized. When a pack would run around, romping and wrestling, instead of joining, Fred would chase them, nipping at their heels and barking incessantly. It was as if he wanted to herd them, but he was coming off too aggressively. A few times, one of the other dogs lashed back at Fred, and I'd have to break up a scuffle. It was never too serious, but it was scary.

Still, I kept taking Fred to the park and watching him closely. I'd never trained a dog before, but I knew Fred needed to be socialized—and he definitely needed time to run and play. Despite the challenges with other dogs, he loved the dog park. Always a bit on the independent side, Fred was happiest off-leash when he could wander around, explore, and sniff everything at his own pace. I smiled to myself watching him bop along with his curly, fluffy tail in the air, still the confident, happy dog I found in Sangin.

Every morning before work, I'd fill up my coffee mug and we'd go out. As Fred got to know some of the dog park regulars, he started to relax a little. The next problem was actually getting him to leave when it was time to go. Even when I'd bribe him with a handful of treats, Fred couldn't have cared less. So, when it was time to leave the park, I started to trick him. Fred loved to cool down in the creek that was part of the park. It was separated by a fence with access through a gate. If Fred wasn't listening to me, I'd go stand by the gate. When he saw me there, he'd come running, thinking he was going to go for a dip. Then right as he ran up, I'd reach down, grab him by the collar, and clip him to the leash so we could go home. He wised up to that pretty quick, and then I was back to square one.

To train Fred to be less possessive of his food, I started taking away his kibble while he was in the middle of a meal, or I'd stick my hand in his bowl while he ate. A few times, he snapped at me. Once when he was chewing a rawhide bone—he *loved* those—I pulled it away from him, and he turned and bit me on the wrist, hard enough to draw blood. I was pissed. I lunged toward him and grabbed him by the scruff, pinning him to the floor. Fred, who wasn't giving up easily, squirmed and yowled. I

CRAIG & FRED   245

held on, holding him in place, saying, "No!" We had it out for a minute, struggling like two brothers. Finally, Fred submitted, letting his body relax. After that, he never bit again.

By the end of the summer, I found one thing that worked well for us: long runs. It helped Fred get used to the leash and it gave both of us a chance to clear our heads and drain our energy.

Fred wasn't the only one who had to adjust to life at home. That first summer—that first year, the first few years, really—I had a lot of my own ups and downs. Making a new life after Afghanistan is a process that's ongoing.

After that night at the bar, when Ysa told me I couldn't hold everything in, I tried to do a better job of opening up with people. It wasn't easy, and it didn't happen all at once. I still worked at the DIA at that point, and one thing that initially helped was talking with one of my coworkers, Jason. He was about my age and was a former marine scout sniper who had served in Iraq and Afghanistan.

Part of my initial resistance to sharing my deployment stories with Jason came from the fact that he had a really impressive military résumé. He'd seen combat in Ramadi and Fallujah, then Afghanistan. In my mind—and I made this assumption all the time with other combat vets—he'd seen way more fucked-up shit than I had. If Jason had his shit together after three deployments, then would he really want to hear about what I'd seen and done on my one combat deployment?

Jason and I fell into a lunch routine where we'd go to the food court and do the usual thing coworkers do: vent about the job, talk about the weekend, blow off steam. But as I slowly started to tell Jason about Sangin—about the nightly patrols, the fire-fights, the rocket, and, eventually, about Sean and Justin—I realized how affected he was by what I was saying. His reactions made me reconsider how much I might have been downplaying what I'd been through. I also realized, flat out, that it wasn't a competition between us.

Later, talking to Tom, my former commanding officer who had helped me get the DIA job, I got a similar reaction. When I told him about how I kept working after my TBI and after Justin, he looked at me and said, "Man, you stayed. You could have gone on a few missions, gotten your Combat Action Ribbon, and come home satisfied. But you stayed out there. You exposed yourself, and you got everything out of that deployment you could have. That's something to be proud of."

Talking to the guys helped me recognize the significance of my deployment. It validated me, and it also made me realize that talking helped. That was a start.

I'd also gotten used to strangers asking about Fred when we were out together. They'd want to know what kind of dog he was—*Is he part corgi?* was a common question—or where I'd gotten him.

I answered honestly. And more often than not, when someone heard me say "Afghanistan," they wanted to hear more. So I'd tell them a bit about the marines, and Sangin, and our mission. Before I knew it, I was talking about war with strangers. I didn't realize it at first, but after coming home from Afghanistan, having Fred helped to keep me from feeling isolated. I met people, and I had a chance to tell them about my experiences in a way that made them feel relevant.

Still, it took me nearly three years to go to the VA. I was

stubborn, and I hated the idea of being coddled. I was physically active: I ran, mountain-biked, played hockey, went on trips with Fred. Occasionally my ears rang, but that was pretty much it. Back at Pendleton, when I'd first gotten home from Afghanistan, I had to show up at the Wounded Warrior center because of my traumatic brain injury. I don't know if the woman I met with was a shrink or what, but she more or less said to me: "You saw combat. You're not the same. You're different now." Naturally, I resented that. Maybe I was worried that if I went to the VA, I'd get the same spiel; I'd be looked at as a victim and labeled with PTS.

At the DIA, though, my boss Kevin pestered me to go and wouldn't relent. He'd known me long enough to have all the important pieces of my story: the rocket, Justin, and even how I'd sort of slipped through the cracks at the Atlanta postdeployment retreat. He was a retired marine colonel, and I think he felt responsible for me and for the way my separation from active duty may have been mishandled.

For the entire time we worked together, and even after I left the job, Kevin stayed on my case. Eventually, I gave in. I got to thinking a lot about a conversation I had with a Naval Academy neurologist on Camp Leatherneck after my injury. The doc was a pioneer of concussion testing procedures for the Naval Academy football team, and he also ran a military TBI recovery center. He was a brain expert. At the time, all I could think about was getting back into the field with the guys, but he sat me down, and he was serious when he talked to me.

"Look," he said, "we know a good deal about what happens to brains upon impact. But you were also knocked out by a blast wave, and we don't know that much yet about how that impacts the brain. The data isn't there yet. You need to keep that in mind."

The doctor continued: "You know how when you drop your laptop, you can pick it back up, brush it off, turn it on, and it still works? But it's not quite the same—it might operate a little slower or freeze up more than it used to. Your brain is like that. Some things are different. We just don't have the resources yet to understand exactly *how* different."

The moral of the story was that I should keep an eye on myself—and let the military keep an eye on me, too. In the years since that conversation, there were times when I'd shrugged off what he said and other times when I thought more deeply about it. Between the pressure from Kevin and the words of the doctor echoing in my head, I finally went to the VA.

Still, I knew going in was going to be a pain in the ass. It takes a full day to be processed, plus follow-up appointments. You get a head-to-toe physical—there's a primary care physician who gives you an exam, an optician who tests your vision, an ENT who checks your hearing, and on and on, including a psychiatrist who checks your sanity.

When I showed up for my first day of appointments, I gave each doctor the rundown: I'm not physically disabled. I'm active. Look, I can even touch my toes! I'm happy. I have no thoughts of suicide. I am fine. And my physical went well: I aced my vision and hearing tests.

My final appointment of the day was with a shrink. *I'll be in and out of here in fifteen minutes,* I thought.

But it wasn't the shrink's first rodeo. He saw right through my BS within the first thirty seconds of our meeting. He was middle-aged, relaxed, and soft-spoken, with kind eyes. He hadn't been in the military, but he knew what he was doing. He asked me about the memorial bracelet I wore for Justin, and before I knew it I was telling him the whole story, even the parts I usually skipped, like my final moments with Justin on the helicopter. I got emotional, but it felt good to let it out.

"Do you think you have PTS?" the therapist asked.

"Probably," I said.

I knew I had symptoms, like hypervigilance and bad dreams. I wanted to be honest, with him and with myself.

It wasn't until a long time later, when I was clicking through the VA's benefits Web site one day, that I saw my diagnosis for the first time. "PTSD—service connected," it read. I wasn't thrilled to see it, but I wasn't surprised, either. I closed the browser without feeling much about it one way or another. All I knew was that I didn't want to let it limit me.

In my second semester at Georgetown, in an ethics course, something clicked. We were assigned to read James Stockdale's reflections on his time as a prisoner of war in Vietnam. The essay, called "Courage Under Fire: Testing Epictetus's Doctrines in a Laboratory of Human Behavior," captivated me. In it, Stockdale recounted how he drew upon the philosopher Epictetus's teachings during seven years of imprisonment and torture. Epictetus was, for most of his life, a slave. Part of the philosophy he created was about how you can't let things that are out of your control determine your attitude. As Stockdale wrote, "What Epictetus was telling his students was that there can be no such thing as being the 'victim' of another. You can only be a 'victim' of *yourself.*" Epictetus said, "For it is *within you,* that both your destruction and deliverance lie."

When I read the essay, I couldn't help but think of Fred. When I found him in Sangin, covered in bugs and dirt, without any buddies or even a source of food or water, he easily could have been aggressive or hostile. But he wasn't; he was sweet. He had no reason to trust me, but he did. Even in a harsh environment, his attitude was stubbornly positive.

When we came home together, Fred was a source of light. If I was pissed off or upset about something, playing with him cleared my mind and made me feel calm. Even simply *looking* at Fred was comforting. We'd been through so much together, and he got it. We were a team.

Yes, I had been through a lot in Afghanistan. Yes, it affected me. Yes, I was dealing with PTS. Because of that, it seemed like people allowed me—or even expected me—to be negative and cynical. Fred not only showed me I didn't have to be that way, but he helped me be better, just by being there. I probably knew it before, but I realized something loud and clear: it's not what happens to you that matters, it's about how you make meaning out of those experiences. If Fred could do that, then I could try to, too.

CHAPTER 17

The Uncertain Path

On a hot afternoon in mid-August, shortly after I got home from the road trip, Josh helped me move into a house near campus. The old, white-shingled row home sat on a small lot with a patch of grass and a porch where I hung an American flag. I didn't have much to move: just a desk, mattress, small fridge, footlocker, and an old thrift-store chair Fred loved to sleep in. I also still had some of Josh's things, too—like the leg he busted in the redwoods—so he was coming to pick them up.

Josh showed up with a clean shave and fresh haircut.

"Well, if it isn't the pig in the silk hat," I joked. I knew he was interviewing for jobs again. No one would have hired him with that on-the-road scruff and stink we'd cultivated.

After lugging the furniture to my room, we sat out on the back porch with a couple of beers. The sun was low in the sky, but it was still hot in that late-summer way. The deck overlooked a small, fenced-in backyard with patches of grass and bricks. Fred moseyed around, sniffing at the ground. Beyond the yard, we could see parents helping their kids move into the college housing units around us. I watched as they hugged good-bye and, one at a time, drove off.

Between sips of beer, we talked about the year ahead, how Josh was back in the application grind, looking for a job, and how I was looking forward to starting classes again and playing ice hockey with the guys. We joked about the trip and how we were proud of it, too. The accomplishment felt almost like being in the military—something only a sliver of people get to experience.

"I feel like an asshole for the things I said in Minneapolis, man," I said, putting my beer down. There was no resentment between us, but it felt important to clear the air. "I was out of line trying to tell you how to deal with your issues."

In our argument, I'd told Josh not to let his injury become the most interesting thing about him. Even though I meant well and didn't want him to get bogged down in trying to prove himself to anyone, I knew my words had sounded harsh.

"You weren't wrong about it," Josh said, bringing his beer to his lips. "I definitely saw what I can do this summer. I know I need to value my time here and not just coast through it."

"We both need to make sure we never forget that," I said.

Looking back on that night, I knew a lot of what I saw in Josh, I saw in myself, too. Neither of us wanted to be looked at as victims because of what we'd been through in Afghanistan. We didn't want assumptions to be made about us. We didn't want to be put into boxes. We'd both had near-death experiences and seen our friends die. We knew we were lucky to be alive. That's why we pushed ourselves so hard. It fueled us and kept us moving forward, but it was also a lot of pressure. Sometimes, we'd get so caught up in being fine, it was hard to admit when we actually weren't. We didn't want our friends and family to look at or treat us differently, but the truth was, some things about us were different. Josh and I were both striving to reconcile that and trying to figure out how to live fulfilling lives after the military. There were no easy answers.

"I think it'll be a long time before we know just how important this summer was," Josh said.

"That's the smartest thing anyone has ever said with a Natty Lite in his hand." I grinned. We lifted the sweaty cans in the air and cheersed them together.

The next spring, I graduated from Georgetown with a bachelor of arts in liberal studies and a concentration in international affairs. It felt good to have that box checked, but I didn't know what I was supposed to do next. My dad said, "You've got a degree now. You need to focus on getting back to work in a stable job with a future." He wasn't wrong, but I grappled with how I was going to find meaningful work. At my old job at the DIA, we had this phrase: "Take your medicine." We were often told by our higher-ups that we should be grateful for our jobs, but we didn't necessarily always feel that way. Our phrase meant "just deal with it"—sometimes, you were going to have to do things you didn't want to do, like sit inside at a computer all day without complaining or hold a job with no clear career track or way to progress. When I graduated, I felt like I needed to just take my medicine again, but when I thought about returning to a conventional job, my heart wasn't in it. I was terrified by the idea of waking up at sixty years old and not feeling proud of what I'd done with my life.

A couple of years earlier, before the road trip, I'd met a girl named Nora. Nora was a musician—creative, outgoing, and incredibly pretty, with a smile that lit up the room. All this time, we'd kept in touch, sharing updates about our lives and checking in with each other. Just before my final semester at Georgetown, we finally got together, and after I graduated that summer, she moved in with me. With all of us under one roof—me, Nora, Nora's dog, Ruby (an energetic little terrier mix who became Fred's little sister), and Fred—the four of us became a family.

Nora, patient and supportive, worked an office job that paid the bills while I tried to figure out what to do with my life. I'd worked at a men's clothing store throughout school and kept that going, since so much of the job was about talking to people, something I enjoyed and was good at. They also let me bring Fred into the store, a big bonus.

In an attempt to be practical, I applied for a job with one of the most respected government contractors in the beltway. The high-profile firm supported the CIA, and the position I applied for was one I would have pulled my own teeth for just three years earlier. Now, though, I wasn't sure what I wanted. They called me, and I went through round after round of interviews. Finally, they made me an offer. Though I accepted it, they informed me that my security clearance needed to be reinstated before they could give me a start date. The clearance had lapsed while I was in school and it was going to take another eight to twelve months for it to be reinstated. In limbo, I waited.

By this time, Josh had gotten a job that seemed perfect for him. He worked for a nonprofit that organized outdoor conservation work for kids. His love for the great outdoors, he said, had been renewed on our trip. When you're in the military, you derive a lot of purpose from knowing that you're in the service of something greater. Josh thought he'd never get that feeling again, but through his work, he said he felt reinvigorated by the opportunity to serve others as well as the environment. I was really happy for him.

As summer turned into fall, I began planning the fourth annual memorial fund-raising event for Justin. I'd started it back in 2013 after Chaz, one of the bartenders at the Pug, suggested it. I used to go to the Pug on the anniversary of Justin's death and drink in his honor. Chaz, hearing me talk about Justin, offered to host a memorial event at the bar if I ever wanted to.

I called Justin's wife, Ann, who still lived in Pittsburgh. I told her about what I wanted to do and asked if she wanted to recommend a charity we should raise money for. She suggested Tragedy Assistance Programs for Survivors (TAPS), a nonprofit that provides grief counseling to families of military members and emergency responders who have passed, regardless of the circumstances of death.

That year, I made T-shirts that said SCHMALLS on the front—Justin's nickname—and had a Bruce Lee quote on the back: REAL LIVING IS LIVING FOR OTHERS. Tony, the owner of the Pug, bought a ton of Stroh's and donated the night's proceeds to TAPS. It was a high point of my year, and each year after that, it became even bigger.

The year I graduated, Justin's parents would be coming to the event for the first time. We'd outgrown the Pug, so I rented out a bigger venue down the block. At Georgetown, I'd joined a cover band called the 50-Year Storm as the drummer, and we were just good enough to hold down a two-hour set. We'd be playing at the fund-raiser. I was anxious but determined to make it a memorable night—the best one yet.

Then I got a call from the firm that had offered me the intelligence job. In addition to reinstating my clearance, they needed me to come in for a polygraph test. They informed me it was scheduled for the morning after Justin's fund-raiser. I knew that after a night like that—full of alcohol and emotion—I wouldn't be in any shape to go in for the test. I called them immediately and asked to reschedule, even explaining that I was hosting an event for a friend who had been killed in action.

"Sorry, but we don't reschedule polygraphs," the representative said plainly. "That's your date."

The fund-raiser was scheduled for a Wednesday night the week after Thanksgiving. It was cold and rainy, and ticket presales hadn't been great. I was nervous. I showed up that afternoon to help set up. We made signs, decorated, and arranged the T-shirt table. At 7:00 P.M., when the doors opened, Justin's parents were the first to arrive. The venue manager, who also happened to be a marine veteran, met them at the door and showed them inside. When he came over and told me they were there, my heart started to pound in my chest.

Keep it together, man, I thought to myself as I walked over. I introduced myself and held out my hand to Justin's dad, John. He was a big guy with a commanding posture and voice. I smiled thinking about how much he looked like a cop, which he was. Instead of the handshake, he said, "No, I'm a hugger," and pulled me in for a bear hug.

Justin's mom, Deborah, who also worked as a cop, was pretty much her husband's opposite: petite and soft-spoken. But, like John, she exuded strength. Her quiet confidence reminded me so much of Justin.

John, who had a Yuengling in his hand, said, "What's with the Stroh's? We don't drink that crap." He smiled at me, and I could tell he was just giving me a hard time—he was sarcastic and quick-witted, just as Justin had been. John proceeded to tell me how, also like Justin, Stroh's had been the first beer he ever drank. It gave him such a bad headache, he never had it again.

When my dad walked over and joined us, the conversation turned to Pittsburgh. I told them how Justin's accent had been the first thing I'd picked up on. As we talked, I could see out of the corner of my eye that more and more people were showing up. Josh was one of the first ones there, followed by a group from the DIA, including my former commanding officer, Tom, and Jason, the scout sniper I used to eat lunch with. PJ came, too, my close friend from intel training who had deployed with me to Sangin, and a big group of my high school buddies. Sarah had come early to help set up, along with my girlfriend, Nora. Ysa had given me a heads-up that he couldn't make it, but he'd spread the word in the EOD community, and I recognized an EOD technician I'd met briefly in Afghanistan coming through the door, along with three of his EOD buddies. Then, just ten minutes before showtime, the entire Georgetown club hockey team appeared, with a bunch of their friends in tow. People from nearly every corner of my life had come together and were gathered all in one place.

Chaz and my sister got up onstage and introduced the band.

We played our first set, lots of feel-good tunes by Phil Collins, the Red Hot Chili Peppers, Sublime, Tom Petty, and, of course, Johnny Cash. In a break after the first set, Tony, the owner of the Pug, took the stage. He lightheartedly teased about how he'd spotted me "drowning at the end of the bar" all those years ago, getting drunk and emotional on the anniversary of Justin's death. That night, I'd been there with Jason, my buddy from the DIA, another combat vet who understood. Then Tony got serious.

"This is one of my favorite nights of the year," he said. "We're all here to think about someone who left us too soon." Then he introduced John, Justin's dad.

"Justin would have been totally overwhelmed with all of this attention," John said with a smile. I smiled, too, thinking about how he was right. Justin hadn't been the type of person who did anything for attention or praise. "But it means a lot to me and my family to see all of you here and to know my son's memory isn't gone. Thank you."

Through tears, I got up and thanked everyone in the room for being there, too. Then we played our second set, and afterward, the crowd moved to the Pug. I spent the rest of the night by John's side, listening to funny stories about Justin as a kid and about his wedding day. Around 1:30 A.M., Chaz poured us two shots of whiskey. I considered putting mine back down on the bar, sliding it away, and calling it a night. Back at home, I'd laid my suit out across the bed in an attempt to be prepared for the polygraph the next morning. Moving forward with the new job made sense on paper: it'd lead to a solid income, a clear career path, and a sensible retirement account. It was the easy choice. It was also the kind of choice I had been wary of my entire life. If I had lived my life up to that point making decisions that way, I wouldn't have joined the marines, gone to Afghanistan, or met Justin. I wouldn't have moved into the city, enrolled at Georgetown, or gone on the road trip. And I wouldn't have Fred. Whenever I looked at Fred, he reminded me what I was capable of. If I could manage to get that little fur ball out of Afghanistan, then what else could I do?

John and I lifted our glasses in the air. "To Justin," I said. We clinked them together and knocked back the whiskey. The difficult and uncertain path had paid off my whole life. I owed it to myself to continue on it.

Throughout the road trip, sitting on the tailgate of the Land Cruiser or around a fire as it crackled into darkness, sometimes I'd pull out my old, clunky laptop and write. In school, I had been doing a lot of academic writing, but I always had the urge to pen something more personal. Maybe to make sense of what I'd been through. I had no idea how to even start putting into words the scope of the war, my experience in the marines, or my time in Sangin. But an easy place to start was with Fred.

So, as Josh and I made our way across the country, in stolen moments here and there, I wrote the story of my dog. I wrote about giving Fred a piece of beef jerky that first day. I wrote about how he followed us on patrols and what he meant to me and the guys in that hellish combat zone. I wrote about how nervous I'd been to try to sneak him onto Leatherneck and about how generous the DHL guys were. I wrote about waving good-bye to

Fred as his plane took off, not knowing if or when I'd ever see him again. Sentence by sentence, the words came flooding out. It felt good. After I graduated, when people were asking me what was next, the truth was, deep down, I knew I wanted to keep writing Fred's story so that I could one day share it with people. It sounded like a dream, but I was determined to make it my reality.

The morning after Justin's fund-raiser, I didn't go to the polygraph test. Instead, I wrote an e-mail. I sent a short version of the story I'd written about Fred to a Web site called the Dodo, knowing they published uplifting stories about animals. Just a few hours later, a woman from the publication called me. The very next day, she published an article about Fred and me, along with a video of our story. People responded. So many shared their own dog adoption stories and sent well wishes and support. I was floored.

Because of that article, a publishing house contacted me with a question: Was I interested in the opportunity to tell Fred's story, from beginning to end, in a book?

It was a cold, gray day in February when Nora and I packed up our apartment and loaded the car. In the backseat, Fred peered excitedly out the window. Ruby—all ten pounds of her—danced around beside him, trying to get a good view. I shifted the car into drive and pulled away from our apartment, through the neighborhood, and onto the highway. North of us, the forecasts called for a blizzard. There was up to two feet of snowfall projected in Maine, which was where we were headed.

I'd been to Maine twice before, though neither time was much of a visit. Nearly all military members fly through Bangor on their way to or from Afghanistan and Iraq. In the airport, a troop of veterans and locals volunteer 24-7 to send off and greet servicemen and women on their short layovers. Maine had been the last piece of the U.S. I saw before I left and the first to greet me when I came back. I wasn't sure exactly what was drawing me back to the state, but I had a good feeling about it.

Nora and I had found a rental house on the ocean, one that had been built by the owner's grandfather, a World War II veteran. All we knew was that the place would give the dogs plenty of room to explore, and that it'd be quiet and smell like the sea. Perfect for writing.

In the car, snowflakes began to fleck the windshield. We took it slow, carefully making our way. In the backseat, we put a pillow between Fred and Ruby so they each felt they had their own little nest. But Ruby, who loved being close to her big brother, ended up asleep on the pillow with her butt resting on top of Fred's. We were listening to oldies and blues. Nora changed the music, knowing it was time for Johnny Cash. I smiled and tapped my fingers on the steering wheel.

In the rearview mirror, I caught sight of Fred, who lifted his brows and looked up at me. I thought about how much we'd been through together. From the time we met, in the unlikeliest of places, to now, we'd had a bond that continually gave me the strength to surmount so many of the challenges that veterans face. Not only did he remind me what I was capable of, but his presence prevented me from ever taking even a moment for granted. Each day, Fred reminded me that a loving, adventurous, and rewarding life was possible if I could continue to choose to be optimistic, even in the face of great calamity or despair. I knew I had rescued Fred once, but Fred continued to rescue me time and time again.

Back in the truck, Fred had that sleepy, happy look, the one he always got when we were on the road together. He had no idea what was next, but he trusted me. It was just the beginning.

For Memorial

In honor of Sean Osterman and Justin Schmalstieg, their parents share their love and memories.

Gunnery Sergeant Justin E. Schmalstieg
MAY 16, 1982–DECEMBER 15, 2010

Since he was a young boy, we knew Justin was destined to be someone special. Justin was noticeably independent at an early age. He was full of life and had a great love for his family, which was evident when his brother John Jr. was born. You could see that instant bond between the two of them. Justin also had a great love and respect for his friends, who in turn showed the same love and respect; he was someone they could look up to.

As Justin grew, he pursued and began dating his one true love, his soul mate, Ann. When Justin graduated high school, he went on to complete one semester at Penn State, then he decided to join the Marine Corps because he said he liked "the way the uniform looked." Several years after joining the Marine Corps, he eventually captured Ann's heart forever, and they were married on November 7, 2009.

Courtesy of John M. Gilkey Sr. and Deborah L. Gilkey

Justin served three tours of duty in Iraq and one in Afghanistan. Throughout his career with the Marine Corps, Justin was known as a comic, but he also had the respect of his superiors and subordinates, and he gave back the same respect until God decided he needed another angel on December 15, 2010.

We are very thankful to everyone, especially Craig, for keeping Justin's memory alive. Not a day goes by without thoughts of Justin. He is forever in our hearts.

Justin's parents,
John M. Gilkey Sr.
Deborah L. Gilkey

Corporal Sean A. Osterman
JANUARY 11, 1989–DECEMBER 16, 2010

With Sean, things always had a flair about them. He was born three weeks late, and at just a day old, he was able to hold his head up. As he grew, he wanted to run, and that's what he did: T-ball, soccer, swimming, lacrosse, karate, and anything that would wear him out. Sean had an active mind, too. He tested at a college reading level in sixth grade and scored 100 percent on his state testing in eighth-grade math.

At age fifteen, Sean was already six feet tall and wanted to join the military. As a junior, he joined the marines in the delayed entry program. He graduated from high school in 2007 and left

Courtesy of Kelly Rae Hugo

for boot camp that summer. Even after suffering a stress fracture in his leg and limping through graduation, he never gave up.

After completing his first tour in Afghanistan, Sean extended his enlistment in order to go on his final deployment. He offered to take the place of a fellow marine who had just had a baby girl with his wife.

When we reached Sean in Germany, we were informed that he was gone but still on life support until our arrival. When we were asked about his viable organs, it's the only time I could hear that baritone voice of his in my mind: "Hell yes, Mom." Sean's organs saved four more people on December 18, 2010. His heart is still beating in Germany, a gift that has sustained us in some dark times.

Sean's mother,
Kelly Rae Hugo

Acknowledgments

Kelly Shetron, coauthor: I am endlessly proud of the work we have done. Thank you for being a consistent and professional coauthor in this effort to share Fred's story. Thank you for helping me make sense of my journey and for shaping it in a way that makes me appear a much better writer than I am. Fred and I are proud to call you our friend.

Chad Luibl, my literary agent and best friend: Your professionalism and tenacity are the only reason our story has received the attention it deserves. Thank you for being my voice and the strongest advocate for Fred and me since day one. In some ways we have come a long way from the playground at Fairview Elementary and our street hockey games in the cul-de-sacs of Burke, Virginia. In more important ways, however, we are still the same. Thank you.

Rachel Kahan, William Morrow: Thank you for understanding from the very beginning how special Fred's story is, and for matching my enthusiasm. Thank you for your expert editorial eye, and for giving me the freedom to work as well as the guidance I needed to work well. And Fred wishes to thank you for treating him like the VIP he thinks he is (and also for the gourmet dog treats you always offer him).

Rosemary Brosnan and Courtney Stevenson, HarperCollins Children's: Thank you for helping me share Fred's story with what is probably his most important audience, and for all the energy, enthusiasm, and joy you exude in our every interaction.

Winnifred Conkling, HarperCollins Children's: Thank you for your hard work and commitment in shaping our story so that it is accessible for a young audience. You have created the type of book I would've skipped recess to read.

Eve Claxton, writing guru: Thank you for your editorial guidance and your ever-positive energy. Thank you for taking the time to understand my story, and for helping me share it in its best form.

And many thanks to Kate Schaefer, Gena Lanzi, Liate Stehlik, Lynn Grady, Kaitlin Harri, Emma Parry, Michael Steger, Eliza Rosenburg, Danielle Kolodin, Natalie Duncan, Alivia Lopez, and the rest of "Team Fred" at William Morrow, Harper-Collins Children's, and Janklow & Nesbit Associates. You all are a part of this, and I am grateful for your hard work.

Honora Parkington, Director of Fred Operations/Girl of My Dreams: You believed in my writing long before you had any reason to. You saw something in me that I thought I had lost, and you helped me find it again. I can't imagine my life without you and I'm so glad that I don't have to. I love you.

Sarah: Thank you for always telling me I was smart, even when I felt stupid. Thank you for never doubting me, even when I doubted myself. Thank you for reminding me that I'll always be your little brother, even though I look so much older than you. And most of all, thank you for helping me sneak a dog out of Afghanistan, even when I thought I couldn't.

Dad: Thank you for being my example of what it means to be a man. Because of you I understand the importance of selflessly serving my community, my country, and the world. You taught me the value of hard work, and you inspired me to become the man I am today.

Mom: Thank you for trusting me, even when it terrified you. Thank you for guiding me when it seemed like I wasn't listening. Thank you for making me laugh, sometimes when there was little reason to. Thank you for always believing in me in those times when I didn't believe in myself.

Nonnie: Thank you for being the toughest and most loving lady I've ever met, for teaching me how to be honest and brave. Thank you for your endless love and support.

Jason B.: Thank you for your dedication to my sister and the wonderful family you two have created. Your work ethic and adaptability are of a superhuman caliber.

Maurice: Thank you for your endless support and for being an example to me of class, grace, and Belgian hospitality. Thank you for loving my family and taking care of my mom.

Bren: Thank you for helping to take care of Fred, and for loving my family and always treating me like your son. Thank you for loving my dad and keeping him young.

Josh: Thank you for coming on the road trip with Fred and me. It would not have been the same without you. Thank you for being an example of friendship and brotherhood. Thank you for all your help with this book and for always believing in our story.

Ysa: My friend and brother, you're the kind of person that I brag about knowing. Thank you for always being a phone call away, no matter how far a distance you might actually be. Thank you for being equal parts goofball and badass. You're an amazing husband, father, and friend.

Bobby: Thank you for getting shot in the arm so you could come and hang out with us in Sangin, and thank you for putting your art career on hold to be a marine for a while. I'm proud to have served with you and I'm proud to be your friend.

Dave: "Thank you for kicking that guy in the chest, and for always letting me sleep in your sleeping bag, and for not getting mad when I hid that donkey leg on your pillow. Love, Fred."

Jason: "Thank you for making me my first collar. Even though I didn't like it, I know you worked hard on it. Thank you for petting me and defending me from those mean guys that day. Love, Fred."

Mark (Top): Thank you for being one of Fred's first friends, and for helping me stuff him into that duffel bag so I could bring him home. Thank you for showing us what it is to be a leader worth following.

Joe: Thanks for your contributions to the book and for being a friend to Fred and me. I am proud to have served with you.

Adam: Thank you for not treating me like an attachment. Thank you for your friendship and for your leadership. I am proud to have served with you.

The marines of First and Second RECON: Thank you for letting me contribute to your mission and for your daily demonstrations of bravery and kindness. I am proud to have served with every one of you.

Tony: Thank you for taking the time to listen to me, even when you couldn't understand me. Thank you for carrying Stroh's even when nobody wanted to drink it. Thank you for helping me honor my friends. I am proud to call the Pug home and I am proud to call you my friend.

Chaz: Thank you for giving me the courage to share the memory and story of Justin. Thank you for listening to me and reminding me what good music is. I can't wait to see how big we can make Schmalls Fest. I'm proud to call you my friend.

Georgetown hockey program: Thank you for giving this old bruiser another shot at glory, and for reminding me how special this game we play is. It is an honor to have won and lost beside each of you. Thank you for your continued support and friendship.

My DIA friends: Thank you for getting water with me every twenty minutes and for listening to my stories about Fred, no matter how many times you'd heard them. Your presence made every day a bit brighter, and I loved working with you.

Bill: Thank you for being my first friend in the marines and for showing me that I could be a marine while still being myself. Thank you for helping me with my school papers and not calling out all the times I swore I'd never go to college.

PJ: Thank you for always believing in Fred's story, for inspiring me to share it, and for helping me see the value in being a writer instead of an intel guy. Thank you for helping me move apartments more times than I can remember.

My friends: Thank you for always treating me the same no matter how different I might feel on the inside. Thank you for standing by me and not being afraid to tell me when I'm wrong. Thank you for being awesome to one another and for only growing up the appropriate amount.

Dog friends: To anyone who has casually asked me "What kind of dog is that?" in a dog park, campsite, street corner, or hotel lobby, thank you for listening and recognizing that Fred is more than a dog to me. Most of all, thank you for not calling him a corgi.

Fred's social media supporters all over the world: We would not be here without you. Many of you have believed in our story from the very beginning. You have provided the support and validation we needed to keep going, and the positive stories you've shared have been a true inspiration. Thank you.